AUDI'S HISTORIC FLEET

HORCH, DKW, NSU, WANDERER, AUTO UNION, AUDI AG

Audi Tradition

AUDI'S HISTORIC FLEET

HORCH, DKW, NSU, WANDERER, AUTO UNION, AUDI AG

SCHIFFER PUBLISHING

4880 Lower Valley Road • Atglen, PA 19310

Audi Sport
HY
itk
12
13

FOREWORD

This book is intended to give a glimpse into the holdings of the Audi AG Historical Vehicle Collection, which are otherwise not open to the public. Currently, in the summer of 2022, the collection, which is spread across several locations, houses an impressive 727 motor vehicles and almost 200 motorcycles. In addition, there are countless small exhibits, such as technical cutaway models, and an extensive archive, whose storage rooms are overflowing, as are various servers on which digital data records are preserved for posterity.

It's by no means a given that this multitude of exhibits from almost 125 years of company history exists today. Unlike some other car manufacturers, neither Auto Union GmbH nor the later Audi NSU Auto Union AG had any ambition to document their product history of two- or four-wheelers and preserve it for posterity. At best, a few well-hidden mementos were preserved by chance in storerooms or in the catacombs of the old factory facilities in the city center of Ingolstadt.

When motorcycle production was discontinued in 1958, Auto Union sold off the remaining stock of its motorcycle-racing department and handed the remains over to the newly founded Zweirad Union, which in turn initiated the disposal. All the postwar DKW racing machines that can be admired today were rebuilt from individual parts purchased from Zweirad Union by a Bayreuth-based car parts dealer! A solitary four-wheeled DKW Front from 1931 had been owned by the factory since 1955, but nothing more.

The situation in Neckarsulm was hardly any better, with the laudable exception of the employees of the disbanded racing department, who preserved and safely stored their NSU racing and record-breaking machines, including a large stock of spare parts, after the factory ended its involvement in racing. Presumably at the instigation of the press department, an NSU car from the brass era had already been restored at the beginning of the 1960s.

Historical files that had been preserved after the destruction of the war and documents from more recent times that were worth keeping ended up in the Neckarsulm factory cellars due to a lack of available archive space. Most of them fell victim to a flood in the Sulm river, which flooded the factory premises at the end of the 1960s. At least NSU, unlike Ingolstadt, had archive regulations in place at the time, which regulated the transfer

Before the mobile museum was built, well-preserved or already restored exhibits were stored in the so-called tire hall. Guests such as Porsche veteran von Hanstein and his wife, seen here, were occasionally given a guided tour of the still very manageable collection.

Treasures showing signs of age, such as the rare and untouched DKW F 1 convertible sedan, for which the original vehicle registration document still exists, disappeared into the sheds until they were restored.

of documents that were no longer required to a central archive and their storage. In the mid-1980s, Auto Union GmbH, which was founded to preserve company tradition and was initially housed under the umbrella of the legal department, began, like NSU GmbH based in Neckarsulm, purchasing vehicles that were important to the history of the four rings. In 1987, the *Ingolstädter Tagepresse* (Ingolstadt Daily Press) stated, "By 1992, the company will have collected 80 exhibits and another 80 vehicles for the reserve. So far, the vehicle fleet consists of 15 motorcycles and 35 cars."

This statement by the then-Managing Director of Auto Union GmbH was made in connection with the revival of an old idea; namely that of a car museum in the automobile city of Ingolstadt. The opening of the State Garden Show planned for 1992 gave new impetus to the museum plans, which had been on the back burner since the end of the 1970s. Nevertheless, it was to be a good ten years before the "mobile museum" was opened.

There was time enough to expand the collection. Over the next few years, the parade of vehicles became more and more extensive; once-spectacular purchases, such as a Horch 780 from the USA, soon faded before the sheer mass of Audi, DKW, Horch, Wanderer, and NSU cars. The founding of Audi Tradition in 1998 transformed the cultivation of tradition into a separate division, which found its home in a newly constructed office building on the periphery of the plant, separate from the legal department. Audi AG's "mobile museum," which opened in mid-December 2002, housed many of the exhibits that had been collected in the meantime in a spectacular setting at the time. The August Horch Museum Zwickau, a joint project of the city of Zwickau and Audi AG, which opened in September 2004, also houses a few items on loan from the Ingolstadt vehicle collection.

Given the large number of model series and derivatives, the current aim is to close gaps in the collection, preserve "typical" engine and color variants for the future, and, at the same time, prepare for electrified or autonomous driving exhibits.

It remains exciting!

Photographer Stefan Warter was commissioned by Audi Tradition to capture the special atmosphere of the vehicle depots. The graphic design of this volume was placed in the capable hands of the Zwickau agency *ö. Konzept*, and Ralf Friese wrote the accompanying texts and the descriptions of selected collection items.

Without the energetic support of our colleagues from the vehicle collection, the various photo shoots in the individual depots would certainly not have gone so smoothly. Join us now on this journey through history.

DKW
DKW

D58H

e-tron
TDI
Power
Great American Roadtrip
Vorsprung durch Technik

THE

EARLY YEARS

The companies founded between 1873 and 1909 that ultimately led to today's AUDI AG were among the oldest automobile and motorcycle brands in the world.

The first motorcycle was built in Neckarsulm in 1900, and it was followed by the first "original Neckarsulm motor car" in 1906. The first car designed by August Horch completed testing in January 1901. In Chemnitz, Wanderer began the production of motorcycles in 1902. In the early summer of 1910, the first Audi Type A left the factory founded in Zwickau in 1909. In 1916, the J. S. Rasmussen Machine Factory in Zschopau experimented with a steam-powered car. In 1919, the first DKW bicycle auxiliary engine built in Zschopau went on display at the Leipzig Autumn Fair, and by 1928, DKW had developed into the largest motorcycle producer in the world.

Audi Type C Alpensieger (Alpine Winner), 1911–1925

Powerplant
Four-cylinder in-line engine, four-stroke

Output
35 hp at 1,700 rpm

Displacement
3,562 cc (217 cu. in.)

Maximum speed
80–90 kph (49.7–56 mph)

Fuel consumption
15-17 liters per 100 km (15.6–13.8 mpg)

Production life
1911–1925

Total number produced
1,116 cars

ALL GOOD THINGS COME IN THREES

August Horch founded the A. Horch & Cie Motorwagenwerke in 1899. In 1920, the company moved to Reichenbach in Vogtland, before finding a new home in Zwickau under the name August Horch Motorenwagenwerke AG in 1904. After a disagreement with the supervisory board, Horch was forced to leave his first company in 1909. In the same year, barely four weeks later, he founded a new company, the August Horch Automobilwerke GmbH, also based in Zwickau.

This newly founded entity immediately met with protests from the Horchwerke. The dispute ended up before the Reich court in Leipzig, and August Horch was prohibited from using his family name for his new automobile factory. The way out of the dilemma was to Latinize his name, and so Audi Automobilwerke m.b.H. was entered in the Zwickau commercial register on April 25, 1910. (Horch is German for "listen," and Audi is from the Latin word for "to listen.")

In the summer of 1910, the Type A, the first Audi automobile, came onto the market. The 10/28hp car was a further development of well-known Horch design principles. It was followed in 1911 by the 10/28hp Type B and the 14/35hp Type C. The first number denotes the so-called "tax horsepower," and the second indicates the effective engine power.

This third Audi model was one of August Horch's best and most sophisticated designs, deliberately designed for good performance. The overhead intake valves were in a pocket above the exhaust valves, which were positioned at an angle in the cylinder block, and this had a positive effect on the engine's performance and thermal properties. The intake and exhaust valves were covered to keep out dust and oil.

Two cylinders were cast together in each block; the solid light alloy crankcase, hermetically sealed off the engine compartment between the frame members at the bottom, housed the de Saxe crankshaft—that is, offset by 14 mm (0.55 in.) from the center position and mounted on three bearings—as well as the camshaft at the bottom and accommodated both bolted cylinder blocks. The engine had pressure circulation lubrication with a gear oil pump, fan-assisted thermosyphon cooling, and dual ignition with a Bosch magneto. A Zenith carburetor supplied the engine with fuel; the fuel was pumped from the fuel tank suspended in the rear of the frame under the pressure of exhaust gases fed into the tank.

The powered rear axle had a spur gear differential—another design detail typical of all Audi models. The thrust was absorbed by a cardan fork. The rather conservatively designed chassis

In 2009, Audi Tradition sent the Alpensieger (Alpine Winner) on the old Alpenfahrt (Alpine Rally) route through Austria, Slovakia, and Italy.

Audi employees from Zwickau celebrated the 1913 Alpine Rally team prize.

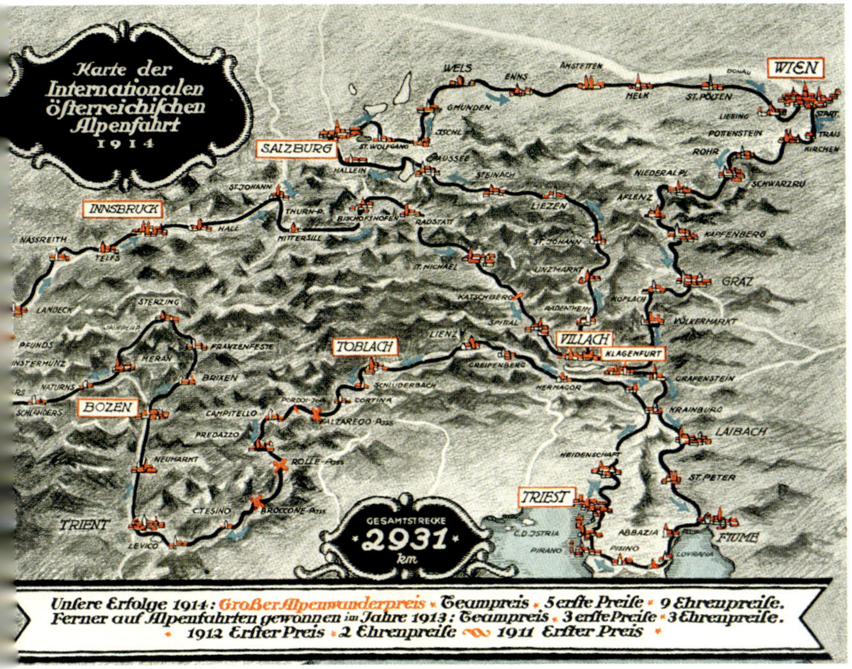

was characterized by a four-speed countershaft transmission with an external splitter gearbox, leather cone clutch, hand-lever-operated inner shoe brakes acting on the rear wheels, and a foot-operated outer band brake acting on the cardan shaft at the transmission output. The top speed of the Type C with a short chassis was between 90 and 100 kph (56 and 62 mph), depending on the year of construction and development status of the engine.

The Type C proved its class when, from 1912 to 1914, it won the Austrian Alpine Rally, one of the most difficult long-distance motorsport races of its time, three times in a row. As Horch and his team also won the team prize three times, the Great Alpine Challenge Cup went to Audi in Zwickau in 1914. This established the Audi brand and its reputation within a very short period of time.

The Alpine Rallies were anything but pleasure trips, which is why there was only time for souvenir photos on arrival and departure and when "putting up" somewhere in Slovenia.

AUTO UNION

The self-supporting wooden bodies of the DKW PS 600 sports car in the foreground and the Audi Type P in the background look like prehistoric skeletons. For stability reasons, the roadster body sitting on the right had only a passenger door and belonged to the DKW F 1, the first vehicle with front-wheel drive to enter large-scale production in 1931.

IN KW58H

Powerplant
Eight-cylinder in-line engine, four-stroke

Output
100 hp at 3,300 rpm

Displacement
4,872 cc (297 cu. in.)

Maximum speed
110 kph (68.4 mph)

Fuel consumption
20–25 liters per 100 km (11.7–9.4 mpg)

Production life
1927–1929

Total number produced
145 cars

Audi Type R Imperator, 1927–1929

THE MAJESTY OF THE POWERFUL CAR

The first Audi model with the prestigious eight-cylinder engine was produced under the direction of chief designer Heinrich Schuh, who had held the position beginning in 1926. The 19/100 PS Type R, together with the Audi six-cylinder Type M18/70 PS, which had been in production since 1924, was supposed to elevate the two-model policy of the Zwickau carmaker to the highest level.

While the frame, axles, and general design of the chassis, with rigid axles, semi-elliptical spring suspension with shock absorbers, thrust ball support for the rear axle, Rudge toothed rims, and Bowen central lubrication system, corresponded to those of the Type M, the designers had "refined" the new engine primarily from a cost perspective. In contrast to the elaborate light-alloy six-cylinder with overhead camshaft, the 340-kilogram (750-pound), in-line, eight-cylinder engine was quite conventional. The long cylinder block with side-mounted valves was made of gray cast iron and was enthroned on a light alloy crankcase in which the five-bearing crankshaft rotated at a maximum of 3,700 revolutions and drove the camshaft, ignition magneto, and alternator via a timing chain.

Eight cylinders, each with an 80mm (3.15-in.) cylinder bore and 122mm (4.8-in.) piston stroke, resulted in a displacement of 4,872 cc (297 cu. in.). With the resulting output of 100 hp at 3,300 rpm, the Type R belonged to the elite "100hp club" of the time. The maximum torque of 28 mkg (202.5 foot-pounds) was already available at 1,100 revolutions per minute and allowed shiftless driving. The engine and transmission were separated by a multi-plate dry clutch, which—according to the advertising—"enabled smooth and shock-free starting." Practically from walking speed, driving took place in the third and therefore highest gear of the manual transmission. On the other hand, those who had the confidence to do so could roar through the countryside at a maximum of 3,700 rpm and 120 kilometers per hour (74.5 mph). Quite impressive figures, especially when you consider that the 5.20-meter-long (17-foot-long) chassis with tires alone weighed 1,550 kilograms (3,417 pounds).

A 19/100hp Pullman sedan had an empty weight of a good 2.1 metric tons (2.3 tons) on the 20-inch low-pressure tires; with the permissible "payload" of 650 to 800 kg (1,433 to

Driving down a lonely country road accompanied by the beguiling eight-cylinder sound provides a beautiful trip through time.

The Type R Imperator was reconstructed from historical photographs, and the existing technology was meticulously restored.

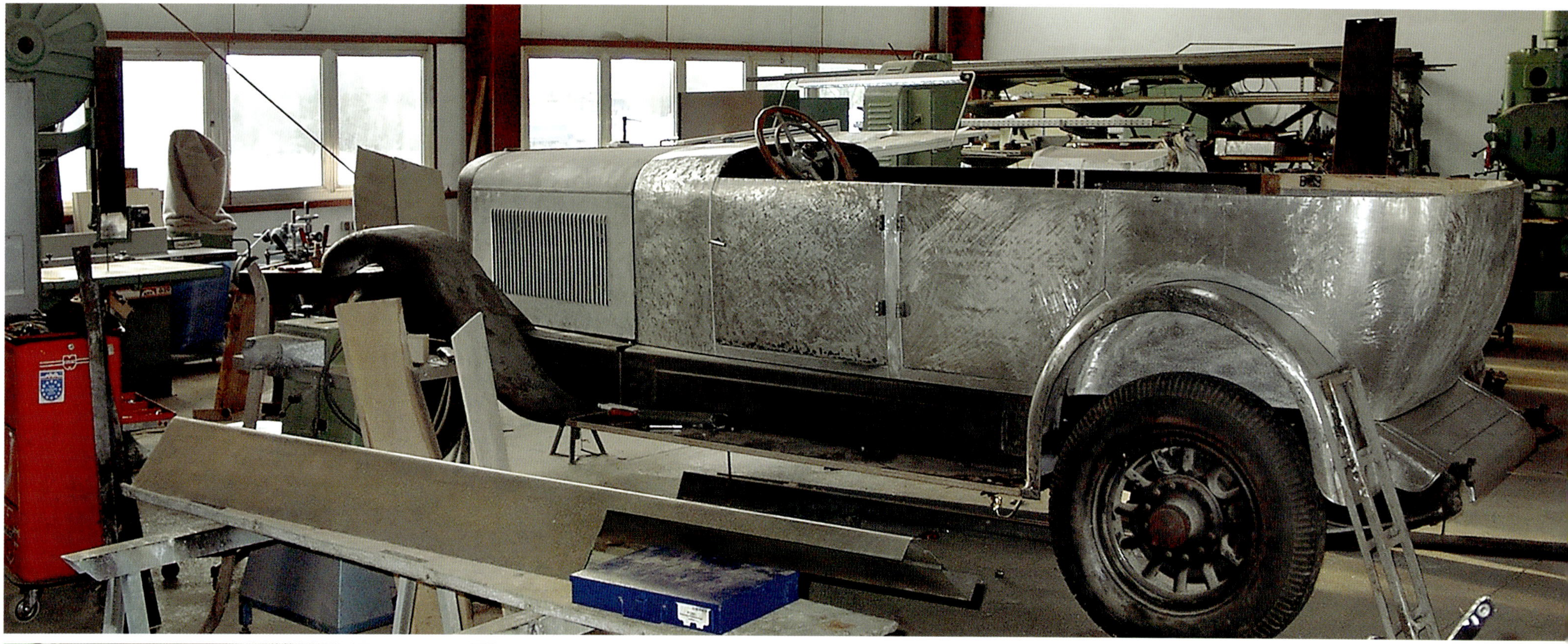

The body of the open touring car is supported by a solid wooden frame. Even the so-called artillery wheels still have wooden spokes between the Rudge hub and the rim bed.

1,763 lbs.), depending on the body, the vehicle mass was at the level of a light commercial vehicle. The Zenith or Pallas rising-flow carburetor, fed by a vacuum conveyor, processed the corresponding quantities of fuel, with the eight low-compression cylinders achieving a mileage of at least 22 liters per 100 kilometers (10.7 mpg). The 120-liter (31.7 gal.) tank in the rear guaranteed an acceptable radius of action.

In view of its majestic size, the Audi Type R was given the nickname "Imperator." The Zwickau carmakers only sold the chassis of their top model, and the car bodies were provided by a good dozen coachbuilders. Although production costs had been reduced by 47 percent compared to the Type M, the Audi Imperator was still a very expensive car; potential customers held back in view of the difficult global economic situation, and only 145 Audi Type R chassis left the production line between 1927 and 1929. The Imperator still appeared in the Audi price lists in 1931, when the last remaining stocks were finally sold off.

Built in 1929, the Imperator in the Historical Vehicle Collection is, with a high degree of probability, the last surviving example of the series. It escaped waves of scrapping for steel production for the armaments industry and confiscation, survived the war by a stroke of luck, and was presumably to begin its second life as a fire engine in the early postwar period. Stripped of its bodywork, the chassis awaited a conversion that was never to take place. It was only decades later, now owned by Audi AG, that it was restored and rebuilt with a historically correct seven-seater touring car body by the Rosenow restoration company in Brandenburg.

Registered and ready to go—probably the last of the 145 Audi Type R Imperator automobiles that were built

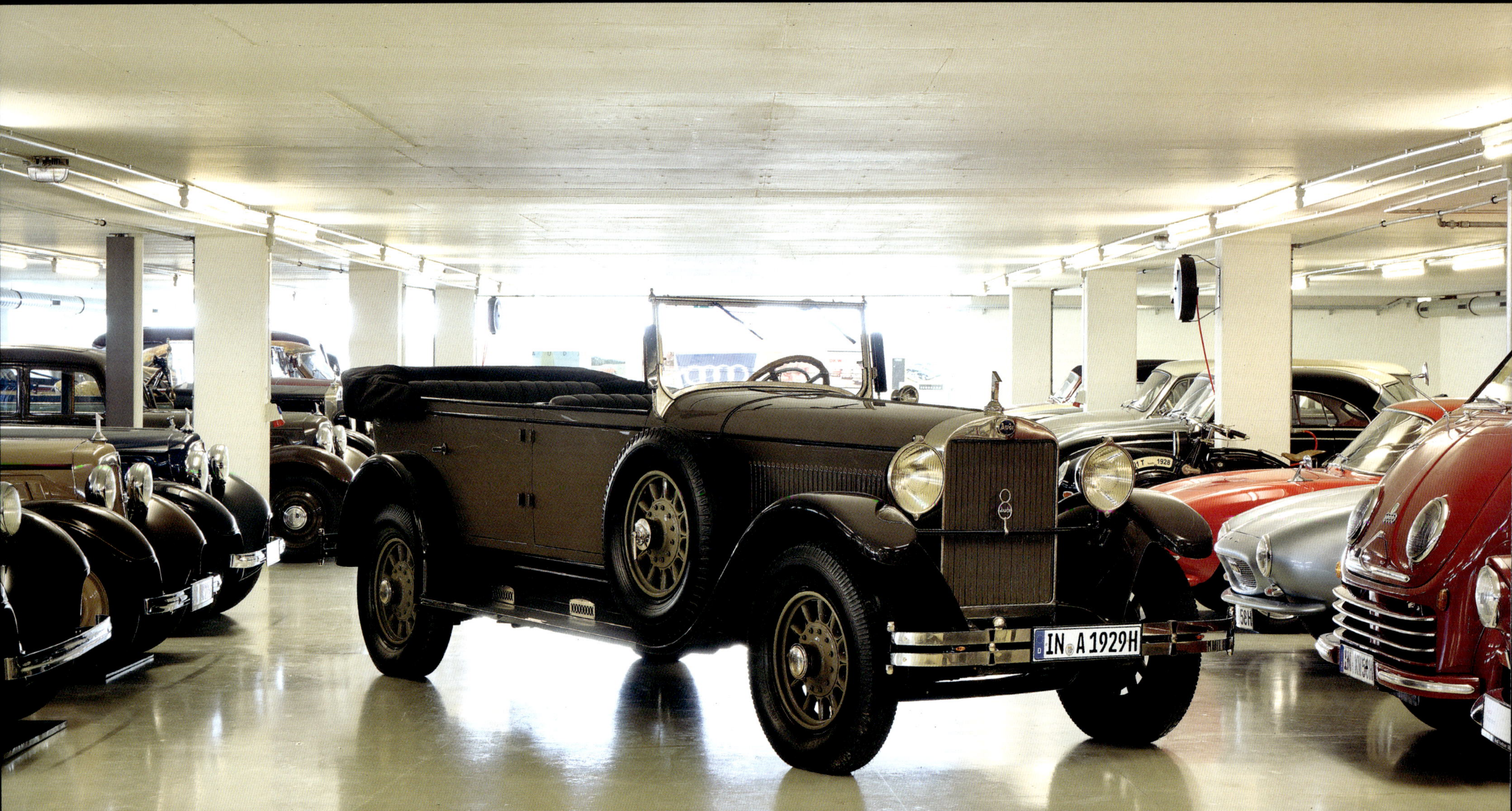

Audi
LITER

Audi

The ignition and fuel/air mixture control levers are mounted on the steering wheel. The switches and instrumentation are in keeping with the style of the time and provide the driver with the most important information.

HORCH

Interior of the Horch B Type 303 from 1927. Even in this luxury phaeton, the driver was "clamped" upright behind the massive steering wheel, with little freedom of movement.

On the right is a row of six Horch eight-cylinders, followed by a Horch 10/50, the last four-cylinder produced by the company. In the background are several examples of the Audi Front and, *on the facing page*, a Wanderer Stromlinien replica. On the left of the photo are various DKWs from the 1950s.

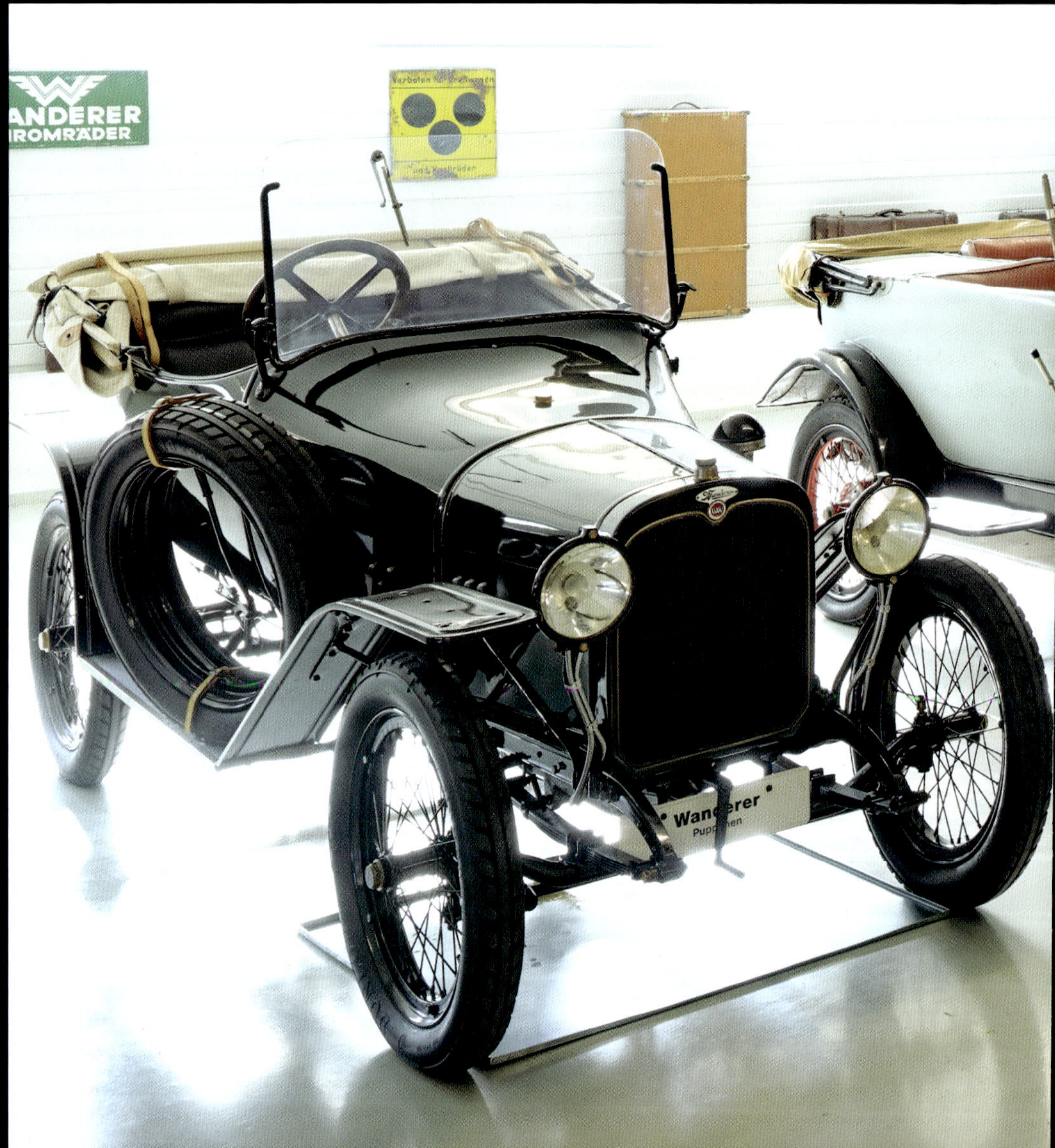

Three Wanderer W 3 5/15 PS Puppchen from the late 1910s and early 1920s. The tow truck was made from a highly elegant Wanderer W 11 Cabriolet—*sic transit gloria mundi* (fame is fleeting)!

Wanderer W 25 K, 1936–1938

Powerplant
Six-cylinder in-line engine, four-stroke with supercharger

Output
85 hp at 4,000 rpm

Displacement
1,963 cc (120 cu. in.)

Maximum speed
145 kph (90 mph)

Fuel consumption
16–20 liters per 100 km (14.7–11.7 mpg)

Production life
1936–1938

Total number produced
259 cars (roadsters and convertibles)

WHOEVER WANTS TRUE VALUE CHOOSES WANDERER

At the International Automobile and Motorcycle Exhibition in 1935, Auto Union AG presented three attractive roadster models from the group brands Audi, DKW, and Horch. The sporty two-seater from Wanderer, on the other hand, was not finished in time and did not make its debut until the following year.

Originally, the development engineers at the Wanderer plant in Siegmar had wanted to use the stock conservative rigid-axle chassis of the Wanderer W21 for their supercharged sports car. In view of the targeted top speed of 145 kph (90 mph) and the known problems with front axle wobble on this chassis, the decision was made to continue the new development with the chassis of the new Wanderer W24 four-cylinder model. The rigid rear axle, which was still installed with a high transverse leaf spring, used DKW patents as a so-called floating axle. The front wheels were suspended from a swing axle with a transverse leaf spring at the bottom and triangular control arms at the top, which also acted as hydraulic lever shock absorbers. Four crossbars and two U-profile plates connected the electrically welded frame.

Auto Union had moved away from the originally planned designation Wanderer W 200 K; at the motor show in February 1936, the two-seater roadster bore its new and final name Wanderer W 25 K. The suffix K stood for *Kompressor* (supercharger), the second reason for the delayed model launch. The technical basis of the compressor engine was the 2-liter (122-cu. in.), light alloy six-cylinder with wet liners and overhead valves developed by Porsche and tried and tested in various models since 1932. It was a solid, reliable unit, but, with an output of just 40 hp, it was anything but a high-performance sports engine. This shortcoming was remedied in an almost brutal manner by fitting a constantly running Roots blower.

Sturdy steel spur gears and a light alloy cylinder head were the main changes to the basic engine, along with the installation of the supercharger drive in front of the clutch bell housing. The most obvious change, however, was the large compressor bolted to the side of the engine between the rising-flow carburetor and the intake manifold. The two-blade Roots blower supplied by Victor Derbuel in Gera was driven from the

Auto-Union race car driver Ernst von Delius at the wheel of a Wanderer W 25 K. Below is a historical advertising photo of the most beautiful Auto-Union instrument panel of its time.

The top photos below show the W 25 cabriolet (convertible); beneath it are the roadster model at left and, at right, a cabriolet high on the steep bank of the north curve on the Avus racetrack.

camshaft spur gear via intermediate gears and a free-running shaft with two Hardy disks. At a rated speed of 4,000 rpm, the engine produced 85 hp. The blades of the compressor rotated at a good 9,200 revolutions, and the bearings and gear wheels of the blower were lubricated by an adjustable Bosch drip oiler; this loss of lubrication, as the oil got into the intake tract, led to oily spark plugs and engine misfires. If exasperated workshops reduced the amount of oil supplied, it was not uncommon for bearing and gear damage to occur on the compressor, often resulting in damage to the compressor drive, camshaft gear, or ignition distributor installed close to it.

The extravagant technology, including a so-called sports gearbox, which was unsynchronized and difficult to shift, was concealed under a breathtakingly elegant roadster body, which was supplied by the Stuttgart coachbuilder Baur. One month after the introduction of the Roadster, Auto Union presented the Wanderer W 25 K Cabriolet (convertible), also with a body from Baur, which for all its sportiness was considerably more spacious and comfortable.

Production ended in July 1938. By then, 104 roadsters, 140 convertibles, and 16 chassis had left the Siegmar plant.

Technical tidbits: the 2-liter supercharged engine with permanently running Roots "wet" supercharger

690-628
19 VIRGINIA 56

AUTO UNION
WANDERER
Werk Siegmar
Type
Wagen Nr.
Motor Nr.

690·628
19 VIRGINIA 56

POLIZEI
Audi
Tradition
Audi Tradition
690·628
19 VIRGINIA 56

For reasons of space, the Wander W 25 K was parked between "youngsters." The supercharged sports car is definitely an eye-catcher there.

AUTO UNION
HORCH
AUTOMOBILE
WANDERER
AUTOMOBILE
KUNDENDIENST
DKW
DKW F 5 Roadster

Left: The DKW Front models were subject to continual technical updating. *From left*: the DKW F 1 of 1931, DKW F 5 roadster of 1937, and the DKW F 2 Meisterklasse convertible-sedan of 1933.

Above: Horch 851 Pullman Sedan and an original DKW F 5 Front luxury convertible

MOOD

OF OPTIMISM

After the end of the Second World War, some automobile and motorcycle manufacturers were able to transition almost smoothly to so-called peacetime production. These included NSU, where 8,822 bicycles and 98 motorcycles were produced in 1945; other companies in the industry, on the other hand, had perished in the chaos of war.

The partially destroyed Auto Union AG plants were confiscated, expropriated, and dismantled, and the company was deleted from the commercial register in 1948. After a few intermediate steps, Auto Union GmbH was founded as a new production company in Ingolstadt on September 3, 1949, and it would continue the DKW brand tradition.

Bruhn Horch, 1953

Powerplant
Eight-cylinder V engine, four-stroke

Output
92 hp at 3,600 rpm

Displacement
3,823 cc (233 cu. in.)

Maximum speed
125 kph (77.7 mph)

Fuel consumption
18 liters per 100 km (13 mpg)

Production life
1940 (chassis), 1953 (body)

Total number produced
1 car

THE FIRST AND LAST HORCH FROM INGOLSTADT

Auto Union chairman of the board Dr. Richard Bruhn did not have a driver's license and had to use the services of a driver for all his car journeys. Before the war, this posed no problems with the large range of Audi, Horch, and Wanderer models on hand; a representative vehicle was always available. The situation was a little more difficult in the early years of the newly founded Auto Union GmbH. From today's perspective, a tiny two-cylinder DKW Meisterklasse (Master Class) automobile driven by a chauffeur seems like real-life satire, and yet, photographs prove that this did in fact take place. For longer journeys, people made do with the train or with "surviving," albeit by then outdated, prewar models.

One fine late summer's day in 1952, a run-down Horch 830 BL Pullman sedan from the last prewar model series was parked in front of the testing department at the Ingolstadt plant. Over the next few weeks, it was possible to observe how the once-luxurious sedan deteriorated day by day on the factory premises, until finally, at the beginning of November 1952, only the "deboned" chassis remained in the yard, awaiting a general overhaul. Most of those who witnessed this process had questioning faces, while a small group of designers, testing staff, sheet metal workers, and upholsterers smiled knowingly.

Long before the skeletonization of the Horch, which was last used as a cab in Munich, the clay model of a classically conservative pontoon body for the modernization of a prewar vehicle had already been created, which skillfully quoted stylistic elements of the 1951 Mercedes 300 but without slavishly copying it. The path from clay model to final drawings was short; as soon as the design drawings were available, model carpenters in the factory's own joinery set about making wooden knock molds for the body components.

At the turn of 1952–53, a veritable slipway was set up in the cramped test workshop on Dreizehnerstraße, on which the first components of the new body were autogenously welded together, starting with the partition wall in the interior. The sheet metal, which had been hand-welded elsewhere, grew together in no time at all to form a voluminous body. The team of Horch bodyworkers who had fled from Saxony to Ingolstadt had proven their mastery once again under incomparably more primitive working conditions than in the prewar period.

In June 1953, Dr. Bruhn received the car for his sixty-seventh birthday as a "gift from the large Auto-Union family," as the company magazine *DKW Nachrichten* (DKW News) proudly

It was a long way from the Ingolstadt South autobahn on-ramp to Al Wilson in Texas, which did not leave the Horch unscathed.

The Ingolstadt test department created a prestigious new body for an executive sedan for Auto-Union boss Dr. Richard Bruhn. The technical basis was provided by an outdated Horch 830 BL from 1940.

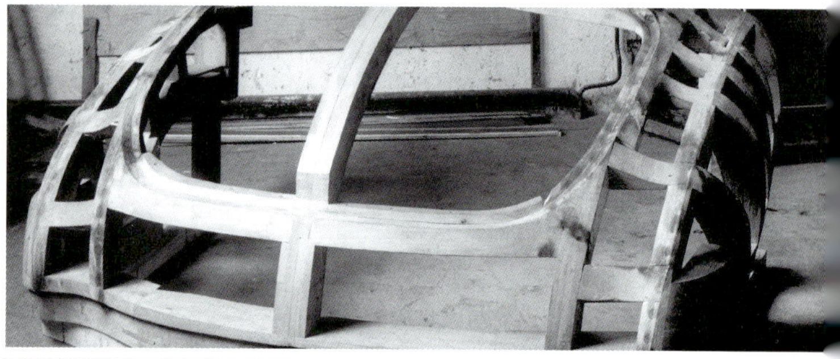

The sheet metal was hammered by hand over wooden models and autogenously welded to form a solid limousine body in the style of the Mercedes 300.

announced. He frequently used the renovated eight-cylinder for trips between the Düsseldorf and Ingolstadt factory sites and occasionally drove it to his hometown of Cismar in Holstein, as the son of the local DKW dealer recalled decades later.

In 1956, Bruhn left the management of Auto Union, which then sold the car—presumably via the Frankfurt branch—to an American soldier stationed in Germany. As the surviving US Forces in Germany license plate from 1957 shows, he continued to drive it in Germany until his service was over and he was able to return home. He took the Horch with him to the United States, where the car was eventually stranded with transmission damage. In 1967, this unique car turned up in a scrapyard, and Texan Al Wilson purchased it for $500. Wilson had the engine overhauled and the defective transmission parts rebuilt. After only 20 miles of driving, the transmission failed again and the Horch was sent to the scrapyard, where it would spend the next few decades. A photo taken in 1967, which was published in the Horch chronicle by automobile writer Werner Oswald, was initially the only vague indication that this car might still exist. Years later, when Audi Tradition received photos from Texas proving the existence of the "last Horch," the story began to move again. Since 2008, the only Horch ever built in Ingolstadt has been part of Audi AG's historic vehicle collection. There is no longer any talk of the restoration that was initially planned; the luxury vehicle, marked by the passage of time, has been allowed to retain the traces of its history and will not be touched.

Framed by a Horch 420 cabriolet from the year 1931 and the Horch 851 Pullman limousine, built in 1935, the Horch 830 BL, fitted with a new body at the Ingolstadt factory in 1953, shows the traces of decades of inactivity.

HORCH

In terms of style, the Ingolstadt coachbuilders were clearly inspired by the Mercedes 300, unveiled in 1951. However, the vehicle's height and tire format show that it is a modified vehicle from the prewar period.

OIL
AMPS
VDO

One of just twenty-five DKW Sonderklasse Zweisitzer luxury coupes built, in original condition. The body was designed by Hebmüller of Wuppertal.

DKW
DKW

The two- and four-seat convertibles are special rarities among the DKW models of the 1950s.

ABUS
A1 open air

DKW StM III, 1955–1956

Powerplant
Two-cylinder in-line engine, two-stroke, air cooled

Output
20 hp at 4,200 rpm

Displacement
500 cc (30.5 cu. in.)

Maximum speed
100 kph (62 mph)

Fuel consumption
6 liters per 100 km (39 mph)

Production life
1955–1956

Total number produced
4 prototypes

MOLLY, MOPPEL, AND THE PLASTIC ALCHEMISTS

As early as 1935, Auto Union AG had developed and produced body parts made of plastic laminate in cooperation with Rommler AG, based in Spremberg. However, a complete DKW body was not built until the switch to Troisdorf-based Dynamit AG, which supplied molded plastic parts for three complete DKW bodies in July 1937. These were mounted on the chassis of the DKW F 7 and later also on the oval frame of the DKW F 8, built from March 1939. Rollover and catapult tests carried out in 1938, 1940, and 1941 showed the clear superiority of the plastic bodies in crash behavior compared to the wooden bodies used by DKW until then. The war and the subsequent peace prevented continuous further development, and series production of a "plastic DKW" never took place.

Employees of the newly founded Auto Union GmbH in Ingolstadt took up the basic idea of a small car with a plastic body that could be produced cheaply. As part of the basic research—which was to be continued at the Düsseldorf plant until it was sold to Daimler-Benz AG in 1961—the "alchemists" based there and initially also in Ingolstadt investigated all known material pairings at the time and developed production processes tailored to them.

The initial impetus for the development of a two-seater microcar came at the end of 1952 from the two-wheeler division based at the Ingolstadt plant. The concept, which was internally referred to as a "motorized four-wheeled vehicle with complete weather protection," was internally nicknamed Molly. An air-cooled 250cc (15.25-cu. in.) single-cylinder engine, derived from the RT 250 and installed in the rear, would have transmitted its power to the rear wheels via a four-speed transmission with reverse gear. The almost 3-meter-long (9.8-foot-long) vehicle, with its trapezoidal shape, weighed a good 250 kilograms (551 pounds) and was supposed to reach a top speed of 75 kph (46.6 mph) with a payload of 225 kg (496 lbs.). According to the cost calculations received, the purchase price would have been DM 2,500. However, the "all-weather scooter" never went into series production, since its creators found it too primitive.

The concept changed radically. Instead of a single-cylinder engine in the rear, the now-two-cylinder drive unit was located in the front of the vehicle and powered the front wheels. The developers expected a power output of around 14 hp from a displacement of 400 cc (24.4 cu. in.). The development, which

The last surviving StM III, photographed immediately after its return from Wolfsburg in the 1980s

Crash tests with the three-seater took place at Manching in Upper Bavaria—if one can believe the captions on an old roll of film. The dismay over the result is written on the faces of Mr. Werner, Mr. von Eberan-Eberhorst, and Mr. Hahn.

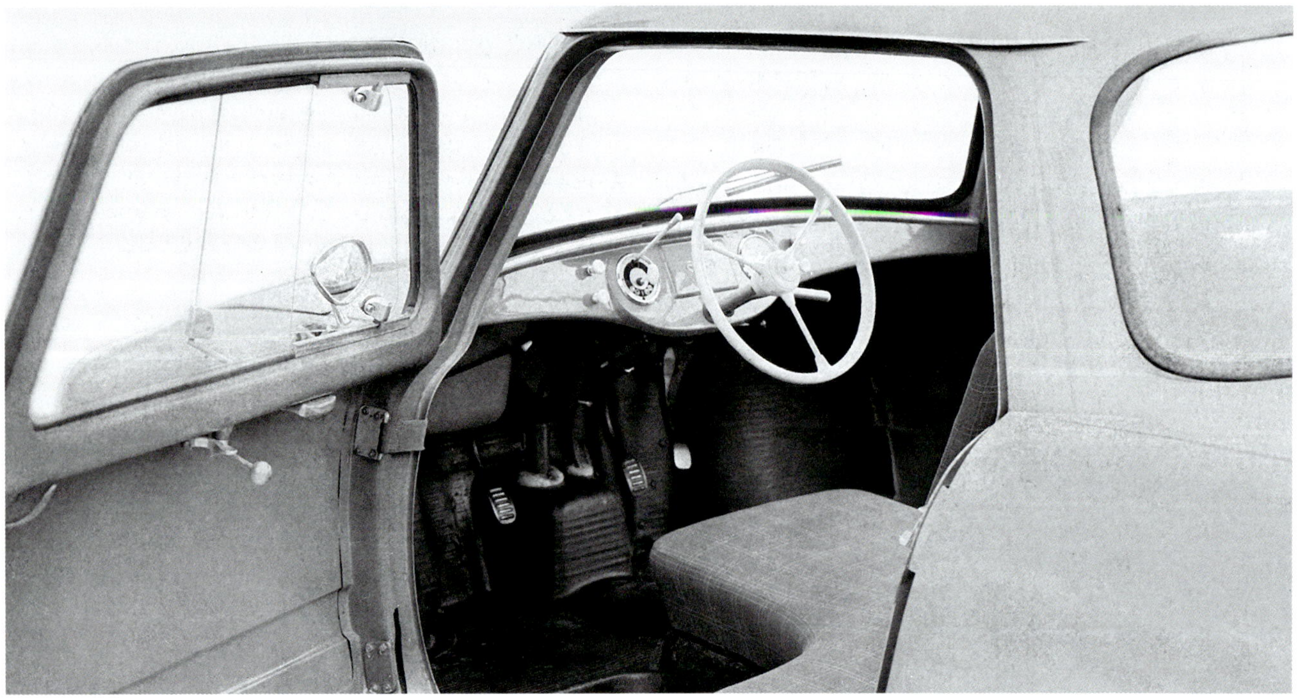

Evolutionary stages of an advanced but not completely thought-out concept

was given the cover designation StM I—"StM" stood for "stationary engine"—was to offer space for three passengers sitting in a staggered position under a hinged roof dome. Even at the model stage, doubts arose as to the customer acceptance of such a folding roof solution. The small car, nicknamed Moppel (Tubby) by employees because of its shape, was to have two proper doors.

By February 1955, the Moppel had mutated into the StM II, with a centrally positioned driver's seat and steering. Its two-door body, made of glass fiber-reinforced DEKADUR plastic, consisted of thirty-six individual parts glued and riveted together and weighed just 80 kilograms (176 pounds). The production of the individual pressed parts took just three minutes, while the subsequent bonding of the individual parts took a good ten minutes. The first test models still had a transversely mounted two-cylinder, two-stroke engine. From 1956, the engine, together with the newly developed gearbox, was installed longitudinally. By June 1956, seven StM IIs in various stages of development had been created as prototypes, and four of them had been tested in endurance runs, after which the decision was made to abandon the three-seater and instead switch to a four-seater model, the StM III, which was already under development. The decisive factor in this decision was probably the clear vote against the three-seater Moppel by the participants of a dealer conference on April 19, 1956.

The first four-seater began road tests on February 6, 1956, powered by an air-cooled two-cylinder engine that had been enlarged to 500 cc (30.5 cu. in.) and now had an output of 20 hp. The decision for the final body shape of the all-plastic body with trunk lid was made on June 13, 1956. The development of all the plastic models had cost around DM 2 million by then, a relatively small sum when you consider the amount of money spent on basic research. The growing uncertainty of the three main shareholders (Flick, von Oppenheim, and Göhner), who were increasingly skeptical about the new technical territory, cast a shadow over the plastics project driven by the head of development, Eberan von Eberhorst, and the bodywork and plastics specialist Kurt Schwenk. At their investigation, on May 17, 1956, William Werner, who had been head of technology at Auto Union AG before the war, was finally brought into the company as an equally skeptical technician and placed in front of Eberan von Eberhorst. The end came quickly and brutally; on September 8, 1956, all development work on the StM III was discontinued on Werner's orders. Just one month later, Eberan von Eberhorst and Schwenk left Auto Union.

A total of eleven STM prototypes were built: seven StM IIs, four of which were drivable, and four StM IIIs, two of which were drivable. The four-seater from the Historic Vehicle Collection had been parked for many years on the inner-city factory premises behind the former testing department and, after the takeover of Auto Union by Volkswagen, was brought back into operation and extensively tested on the Wolfsburg test track. A DKW off-road vehicle with a plastic body turned up in Austria in 2009 as further evidence of plastic development under the sign of the four rings and is now also part of the AUDI AG collection.

On special occasions, the only survivor from the largely unknown DKW StM series of prototypes is taken out of the depot and moved into the public eye.

MÜNCH 4
AB 37 3771

Plastic body, innovative design details, and relatively large interior and trunk spaces elevated the DKW prototype above the majority of small cars of the 1950s.

AB 37 - 3771

The Düsseldorf and Ingolstadt DKWs of the postwar period are very well represented in the museum and collection, with examples of every series and almost every model variant.

BELCAR
S

F5110
F4085
5092

The palette of utility vehicles and vans extends from DKW three-wheel transports from the year 1928 to the Spanish DKW Imosa with Mercedes diesel engine built in 1967.

NSU Prinz II E Wankel Engine 1960–1962

Powerplant
Single-disc rotary piston engine, liquid cooled

Output
30 hp at 6,000 rpm

Displacement
250 cc (15.25 cu. in.)

Maximum speed
Unknown

Fuel consumption
Approx. 10 liters per 100 km (23 mpg)

Production life
1960–1962

Total number produced
3 cars

PRESENTING THE ROTARY ENGINE

For NSU, 1957 marked the beginning of a new era. The two-wheeler era was coming to an end, and as prosperity grew, so did people's demands for comfort, safety, and convenience. For the first time since automobile production ceased in 1929, another passenger car was built in Neckarsulm. Extensive development work had preceded the start of series production, and on August 30, 1957, a four-seater vehicle with a self-supporting body and a fixed engine was presented to the press. At a price of DM 3,739, the four-seat Prinz (Prince) finally arrived at NSU dealerships on March 4, 1958.

February 1, 1957, was another memorable day for the small specialist team of NSU technicians. The first rotary piston engine was made to run on the test bench of the NSU research department. With a chamber volume of 129 cc (7.9 cu. in.), the test engines produced an impressive output of 29 hp at 17,000 rpm. For several years, Neckarsulm had been working on the development of a completely new engine concept: an engine that developed its power not via pistons, but via a triangular rotating rotor (trochoid).

The idea was the brainchild of the technical autodidact Felix Wankel, who had found a partner in NSU-Werke for its implementation, but it was to be a laborious journey from the idea to series production. In the end, it took until 1963 before the NSU/Wankel engine could be installed in the NSU/Wankel Spider as a production-ready power unit.

On February 1, the prototype of the Wankel engine completed its first test run on the engine test bench. The engine worked as a four-stroke without valve control, with the rotating rotor enlarging or (when compressing the gas mixture) reducing the combustion chambers in an eccentric movement. The original rotary engine devised by Wankel concealed highly complicated inner workings: The rotor rotated around not only its own axis, but also the trochoid that surrounded it. It was the head of the NSU research department, Dr. Walter Froede, who can be credited with the decisive simplification of the engine. According to his ideas and suggestions, the rotary engine was turned into the circular or rotary piston engine through "kinematic reversal": In this concept, the outer rotor—essentially the housing—is stationary, and only the piston rotates.

On January 19, 1960, NSU presented the results of its research into the NSU/Wankel engine to the public at a VDI conference in Munich. On this occasion, a rotary piston engine with a

Through a process of "kinematic reversal," the rotary engine on the left was turned into the first rotary piston engine under Dr. Walter Froede.

chamber volume of 250 cc (15.25 cu. in.) demonstrated the functionality of the new engine concept in the parking lot in front of the conference venue. Later test drives and trials under approximate production conditions took place in the shells of three slightly modified NSU Prinz IIs and a Sport-Prinz, all of which were on the road as "mobile test benches." Under constantly changing loads in road traffic, the operating behavior and weak points of the 30 hp KKM 250 engines could be determined without attracting much attention.

The early rotary engines were tested on the road in this sort of inconspicuous housing. As soon as the first details were "leaked," a kind of technical gold-rush mood broke out in the automotive industry. A little later, NSU negotiated its first license agreements.

Slightly tattered, the test vehicle survives to the present time. Someone at the NSU plant, who unfortunately remains unidentified, did not have the heart to scrap it.

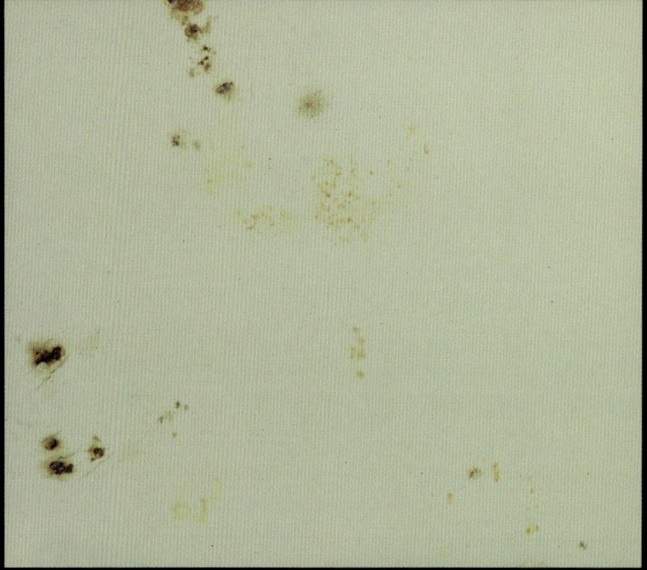

Under the hood, in addition to the KKM 250, are "borrowed" engines from Fiat, VW, and Bosch. The rev counter, which reaches up to 12,000 revolutions, is also remarkable. Depending on his mood, engine boss Roder referred to the early rotary engines in his broad Middle Franconian dialect as "ancient Egyptian water mills" or "gurgling dumplings."

VDO
20 40 60 80 100 120
KM
67138
40 60 80 100 120
0 20
x100
U/min
2683244

Princes in racing trim—the Autonova GT, Wankel Spider, Thurner, TT, and TTS—more than anything, one would love to take them all out onto the track.

NSU

NSU Wankel Spider
NSU Wankel Spider

74H
HN SU 181H
HN SU 590H
HN SU 235H

NSU RO 80

NSU Sport Prinz
NSU Prinz 30

NSU
Ro 80 Auto des Jahres 1967

Brand faces through the decades. The classic, timeless NSU Ro 80 designed by Claus Luthe back in 1963 takes center stage.

NSU Prinz 4

The Prinz 4 and Ro 80 were to be the last vehicle models to bear the NSU brand name and were produced until 1972 and 1977, respectively. In 1985, Audi NSU Auto Union AG was renamed Audi AG, and NSU finally disappeared. The name lives on in NSU GmbH, which was also founded in 1985 to preserve the company's traditions.

NSU Uruguay P6, 1969

Powerplant
Two-cylinder in-line engine, four-stroke

Output
55 hp at 5,500 rpm

Displacement
1,177 cc (71.8 cu. in.)

Maximum speed
120 kph (74.5 mph)

Fuel consumption
6.5–7.5 liters per 100 km (31–36 mpg)

Production life
1969–1971

Total number produced
Approx. 500 cars

SQUARE. PRACTICAL. GOOD?

At the beginning of 1968, Quintanar, the NSU importer in Montevideo, Uruguay, started production of a station wagon using technical components from the two-cylinder NSU Prinz 4 model. In December 1968, Quintanar boss Soler was able to announce the completion of 140 units of the rather rustic rear-wheel-drive vehicle. At the invitation of the NSU management, Soler had traveled to Germany together with the owner of the Chilean company Federic Saci to discuss in Neckarsulm the possibility of switching production to the four-cylinder engine of the NSU 1000 or the technology of the NSU 1200.

While the drive unit of the Prinz 1000 could be easily accommodated in the rear of the station wagon, the conversion to the chassis of the NSU 1200 would have been too labor-intensive and costly due to its modified front axle. In this case, Soler planned to launch a new model on the market straight away. For Chile, the local importer reckoned that the higher-displacement 1200 engine would improve sales opportunities, and planned this conversion as part of its marketing strategy.

The assessment of the submitted design documents by NSU engineers was surprisingly positive, even though the body structure was considered far too complex in some areas, such as the doubled floor panel. In Uruguay, on the other hand, they wanted to be sure that the car could cope with the conditions and loads there. Dr. Wenderoth and Ewald Praxl from NSU were critical of the higher stress on the rear axle caused by the axle load distribution, the limited usability of the cargo space, and the high thermal load on the engines.

The last point coincided with the experience of the importers. At their request, the station wagon received an additional oil cooler from the NSU TT 1200. Compared to the NSU 1000, the vehicle's empty weight had increased by almost 90 kilograms (198 pounds), while the permissible gross weight had only been raised by 80 kg. By increasing the permissible axle loads by 40 kg (88 lbs.) each, NSU was able to permit a payload of 390 kg (860 lbs.) for the station wagon with a clear conscience.

In 1969, Quintanar delivered a "bare" sample body to Neckarsulm, where it was completed with the technology of the NSU 1000 at the factory and sent to the LBF in Darmstadt for testing. There, the station wagon was assessed quite positively, apart from a few "easily remedied complaints." Technical Development Neckarsulm, on the other hand, criticized poorly closing doors

N o t i z

Besprechung bei TC 3 vom 20.Februar 1970

Betreff: Uruguay-Fahrzeug

Konzept der besprochenen Punkte:

- Karosserie selbsttragend als Kombiversion, jedoch wegen Heckmotor hintere Ladefläche nur bedingt benutzbar.
- Die Kühlung des Motors ist unter den klimatischen Bedingungen Südamerikas nicht voll ausreichend. Auf Wunsch unseres Importeurs werden die Motoren deshalb mit einem zusätzlichen Ölkühler (vom NSU TT 1200) ausgerüstet.
- Gewichte:

	Uruguay-Fahrzeug	NSU 1000	NSU 1200
Leergewicht	730 kp	640 kp	720 kp
Zulässiges Gesamtgewicht	1120 kp	1040 kp	1140 kp
Zuladung	390 kp	400 kp	420 kp
Zulässige Achslasten			
vorn	500 kp	460 kp	520 kp
hinten	6[illegible]0 kp	580 kp	620 kp

Das in Neckarsulm stehende Musterfahrzeug wurde bei LBF Darmstadt getestet und abgesehen von einigen leicht zu behebenden Beanstandungen positiv beurteilt.

Seitens TC Neckarsulm werden folgende Punkte bemängelt:

- Schlecht schließende Türen und Hauben.
- Verbindung von Scharnieren zur Karosserie zum Teil mangelhaft.
- Kofferraum und Fußraum eingeengt durch kastenförmige Radläufe und doppeltes Bodenblech.
- Verschiedene Schweiß- und Lötverbindungen mangelhaft.
- Verschiedene Ausstattungsmängel, Mxkxxxxxxxxx
- Motorraum zur Kabine ungenügend wärmeisoliert und nicht ausreichend schallgedämmt.
- Sitzausführung und Komfort ungenügend.

Die angeführten Mängel beruhen auf eine Beurteilung des Musterfahrzeuges, sie sind sicher nicht representativ für die Fertigung in Uruguay. Allerdings liegen uns hinsichtlich der tatsächlichen Produktionsqualität zur Zeit keine Informationen vor.

Neckarsulm, 20.Februar 1970
TO 7: Ta/he

Taufer

In South America, the Quintanar Company aggressively promoted the station wagon with NSU genes, which was largely unknown in Germany.

and hoods, poorly executed hinges, inadequate welded and soldered joints, equipment deficiencies, poor noise damping, inadequate seats, and the constricted front footwell due to angular wheel arches and double floor panels.

The list of defects was followed by the qualification that a few of the weak points criticized on the sample vehicle were certainly not symptomatic of production in Uruguay, but that no information was available on the actual production quality. Until 1971, around 500 four-cylinder station wagons rolled off the production line at the Nordex body construction company, after which the South American adventure ended almost as abruptly as the production of the air-cooled NSU models in Germany following the withdrawal of Neckarsulm from this sales region.

Audi

Rectangular, as if drawn with a ruler, yet barely longer than a DKW off-road vehicle—you cannot miss the NSU Uruguay station wagon. It simply catches the eye from afar.

NSU

PaterNoster

PROGRESS THR

OUGH TECHNOLOGY

Audi NSU Auto Union AG, which was the result of the merger of Auto Union GmbH and Neckarsulmer Motorenwerke AG in 1969, produced a veritable fireworks display of new models in the years that followed its foundation. In January 1971, the advertising slogan “Vorsprung durch Technik” (“Progress through Technology”) appeared for the first time, intended to communicate the diversity of the model range resulting from the merger. With the introduction of the Audi quattro at the latest, the slogan could be experienced in the literal sense of the word.

Two generations of the Audi 80—a first-generation facelifted Audi 100 and a 100 Avant from the third series—share the increasingly limited space with the Audi ASF twelve-cylinder show car and a standard production aluminum Audi A8.

Audi 100
A4 Cabriolet

For reasons of age, the automobile's first owner from Kehl parted with his first and only car in late summer 2018. As a railway worker, he was allowed to travel by train free of charge and had therefore driven the Audi 50 just 32,604 km. The completely original "Smurf" was carefully made ready to drive again but remained untouched visually, right down to the fire extinguisher, lambskin seat covers, and stickers.

EUROTEC
Continental
IN-O 9200
BAVARI
FEUERLÖSCHE
ICH KANN HE
BUNDESVERBAND für den SE
BVS
10
DEVK
VERSICHERUNGS GRUPPE
über 10 Jahre schaden

Audi 100 5D World Tour, 1978

Powerplant
Five-cylinder in-line engine, four-stroke diesel

Output
70 hp at 4.800 rpm

Displacement
1,986 cc (121 cu. in.)

Maximum speed
150 kph (93 mph)

Fuel consumption
10 liters per 100 km (23.5 mpg)

Production life
1978–1982

Total number produced
55,613 Audi 100 5D limousines

AROUND THE WORLD IN SIXTY-SIX DAYS

In October 1978, Audi unveiled the Audi 100 5D, the brand's first vehicle powered by a diesel engine, at Friedrichsruhe Castle near Öhringen. The five-cylinder swirl chamber engine developed at Volkswagen had a displacement of 1,986 cc (121 cu. in.) and produced 51 kW (70 hp) at 4,800 rpm; maximum torque was 129 Nm (95 ft.-lb.) at 3,000 rpm. The Audi, which was consistently designed according to lightweight construction principles but still weighed over 1,200 kilograms (2,645 pounds) as a diesel, accelerated to 100 kph (62 mph) in 17.5 seconds. With a seemingly endless run-up, a top speed of just over 150 kph (93 mph) was achievable. The optionally available three-speed automatic gearbox neutered the acceleration values even further but surprisingly had no effect on the car's top speed.

To prove the performance and reliability of the first Audi diesel vehicle, a special demonstration was considered in the run-up to the press event. Jörg Bensinger, head of road testing at Audi, came up with the idea of a demonstration drive around the world and, since he was responsible for the traditional summer and winter test drives, was able to plan this with his staff.

The following were selected as participants: Bodo Grosch, freelance journalist; Toni Hauf, one of Bensinger's best mechanics; Egon Burow, technician and diesel five-cylinder in-line engine specialist at VW; and Hans-Joachim Grabe, also a technician in Wolfsburg, who replaced Burow for the second part of the trip from Australia. They were joined by Bensinger, by his own admission a "restless spirit with a dash of adventure in his blood."

The preparations in times before the internet or satellite navigation cost time and nerves, since it was necessary to book maps and travel guides, ship passages, and charter flights for the leap from continent to continent; to apply for visas; and to set up a tight schedule that had to be adhered to at all costs.

At the same time, the two Audi 100s were prepared for long-distance driving. In addition to the standard rough-road package, the fuel tank was given underprotection, the strut

The route for the diesel trip around the world, selected by the head of the driving experiment, Jörg Bensinger. Here, he can smile again after stress-filled weeks.

Except for the photo of the departure from the technical development department in the Ingolstadt factory, which was staged after the fact, all the remaining photos are genuine and were not staged.

domes were double-reinforced, and brake and fuel lines were moved to the interior. Instead of the bumpers, there was a massive cow catcher at the front of the vehicle, to which a sand sheet was also attached, and at the rear a sand plate was attached, which could also serve as an impact element in an emergency.

On August 21, 1978, at five o'clock in the morning, two upgraded Audi 100s took off from the Technical Development yard at the Ingolstadt plant without much fuss and without much fanfare. Sixty-six days were allotted to cover the calculated 30,500 kilometers (19,000 miles), because on October 25 the world travelers had to be back in Öhringen for the presentation of the Audi 100 5D to journalists and the international motor press.

The first leg of the trip led via Austria and Yugoslavia to Greece. From there, the journey continued via Istanbul to the Iranian border, which was reached on the morning of August 25. On August 28, the Afghan border was crossed, on the thirtieth the border with Pakistan was reached in front of the Khyber Pass, and only one day later, the entry into India was imminent. The travelers flew to Bangkok, shipping the cars by cargo plane. For the subsequent 2,600 kilometers (1,615 miles) to Singapore, only 48 hours of driving time remained. Two full days had been needed at the airport to complete all the formalities and to be able to pick up both Audis again. After 36 hours of continuous driving, the travelers went through customs in Singapore. The very next day, the cars were loaded into the plane again, and the cars and crew took off at 10 p.m. in the direction of Darwin, Australia. From there, they crossed the Australian continent in seven days in order to fly from Sydney to Santiago de Chile.

On the overland route to Argentina, crossing the Andes was the next major challenge; from Buenos Aires, the route led via Montevideo in Uruguay to Brazil. On the way to the border, the only major accident occurred during the entire trip. One of the two cars lost the left front suspension on the rammed curb after a spectacular evasive maneuver. Since the required spare parts were not available, the suspension strut had to be provisionally welded, and the bent wishbone had to be warm-straightened in a forge. On October 6, the battered and weary travel group was finally able to enter Brazil.

Five days later, a Lufthansa cargo plane brought the expedition to Lagos in Nigeria, with a stopover in Dakar. Before the journey to Niger and the subsequent crossing of the Sahara, all nonessential items had been cleared out of the vehicles; water and diesel supplies took their place. The 1,300-kilometer (810-mile) drive to the border began and, the following day, continued northward on the washboard roads of the Sahara. After 470 kilometers (292 miles), the team reached Agadez in scorching heat. After Agadez, the sand tracks began, and the following 250 kilometers (155 miles) could only be mastered with countless uses of shovels, sand plates, recovery aids, and pneumatic lifting bags. Intruding sand forced a clutch repair, which threw the schedule into disarray, as did customs difficulties when crossing the border into Algeria. After six and a half hours of driving at an average speed of 60 km/h (37 mph), the corrugated iron road to Tamanrasset was conquered, and behind "Tam," there was a well-developed asphalt road to El Golea, heading north. Apart from the sanded clutch and screws that vibrated loose and were then lost, there had been no damage to either Audi. The technology had reliably held out, even at unexpectedly high outside temperatures.

The final spurt began on October 22 with a 600km (3,750-mile) journey across the Atlas Mountains to Algiers, from where two separate ship passages to Marseille had been booked for October 23 and 24 to be on the safe side. The French ship, however, was on strike and remained in port. The second, sailing under the Algerian flag, left on the twenty-forth with a two-and-a-half-hour delay and then headed for Barcelona instead of Marseille. On October 25 at 9.45 a.m., both Audis were finally unloaded and set off for France as quickly as possible, disregarding all traffic rules. In Avignon, the two technicians who had flown ahead from Algiers to the original destination port of Marseille were collected. At 9 p.m., the world travelers reached the German border at Mulhouse, and at 11:53 p.m., they arrived at Friedrichsruhe Castle near Öhringen for the press reception.

In 66 days of travel, each team spent 40 days on the road with a daily driving average of 770 kilometers (478 miles). The consumption of diesel fuel, despite overloading and tortuous driving conditions in the desert, was 10.2 liters per 100 km (24 mpg), plus the engine oil consumption of 0.2 liters per 1,000 km (0.012 liters per mile).

IN-NM8
Audi 100 5D WELTFAHRT AUF CONTI.
Continental

Cow catchers, sand plates, and a raised chassis were part of the preparations for the world trip in the brand-new Audi 100 with five-cylinder diesel engine, which can be seen at first glance.

Two vehicles from Ingolstadt circled the world and, even without satellite navigation and radio telephony, arrived just in time for the model's world premiere in Friedrichsruhe Castle near Öhringen.

Shell
HELIX

The world record car is almost unnoticeable next to the production model. Have you already spotted the two TT show cars, the six-door Audi A3 convertible, or the TT with mid-engine among the parked vehicles?

HB AudiTEAM
Great American Roadtrip
TDI
IN-NR 11

The second, third, and fourth rows of parking belong to the show cars and studies. The convertible show car from the IAA 1988 can be found here, as can the drivable chassis of the Audi quattro Spyder or the Audi Nanuk quattro from earlier days.

Audi
Tradition

A brand-new bodyshell for the Sport quattro was found, thirty-five years after the end of production, safely stored and well protected, in the middle of the factory in Ingolstadt.

IN UQ 82H

The Ur-quattro and Sport quattro are icons that were collected or purchased in good time. Some "short ones" found their way directly into the vehicle collection in the late 1980s, including the first Sport quattro ever built, which had previously been in the service of the press department.

Audi Research Car, 1981

Powerplant
Four-cylinder in-line engine with exhaust-driven turbosupercharger

Output
110 hp at 5,700 rpm

Displacement
1,600 cc (97.6 cu. in.)

Maximum speed
Approx. 180 kph (132.8 mph)

Fuel consumption
8 liters per 100 km (29.4 mpg)

Production life
1981

Total number produced
2 prototypes

FOR THE SAKE OF THE ENVIRONMENT: AUDI FOR THE FUTURE

In 1978, the Federal German Ministry of Research and Technology launched a research program to promote the development of motor vehicles that were more efficient than previous vehicles, particularly in terms of saving energy and raw materials. The aim of the program was to develop vehicles with clear advantages over previous vehicles, particularly in terms of energy and raw material savings, environmental friendliness, and economy, and to make them suitable for mass production. Audi was one of three German car manufacturers to take part in this project.

The aim of the Ingolstadt engineers was to show that advanced technology makes an economical and environmentally friendly vehicle in the upper middle class possible. This was achieved, on the one hand, by designing an aerodynamically optimized body whose drag coefficient was 0.30, and, on the other hand, by using a turbocharged four-cylinder carburetor engine, which was designed for high performance at low engine speeds to reduce fuel consumption. The “wet” turbocharger, located between the carburetor and the intake duct, which prepared the mixture supplied by the carburetor in a particularly homogeneous manner both mechanically and thermally, was not entirely uninvolved in this characteristic. This meant that the finest fuel droplets were better converted into a gaseous state. The lean operation possible in this way led to extremely low consumption and pollutant values.

The aerodynamically sophisticated body boasted a flush, bonded windshield and rear window as well as flush-mounted crank windows. The steel safety cell was specifically crash-optimized and featured bolted light alloy fenders and a bonded sandwich roof. The vehicle floor consisted of a one-piece fiber composite sandwich panel with a polyurethane hard foam core and included the door sills, which are always particularly susceptible to corrosion in conventional bodies. Pre-assembly, including the installation of floor carpets, cables, and seats, could be carried out outside the vehicle. The complete assembly was then fitted into the body structure from below in one piece!

The drivetrain components were in a sound-absorbing enclosure, which was covered by the specifically deformable aluminum sandwich engine hood. Only the radiator was located outside the engine enclosure. Thanks to these measures, external noise could be reduced almost to the noise made by the tires. Airbags, three-point seat belts, knee pads, an integrated child seat, and reinforcements, as well as protective padding in the doors, were used for passive safety.

The concept of a small-volume, supercharged engine was ahead of its time, as was the idea of engine encapsulation to suppress noise emissions.

The Audi BMFT research car anticipated many ideas incorporated into the third generation of the Audi 100, unveiled in 1982.

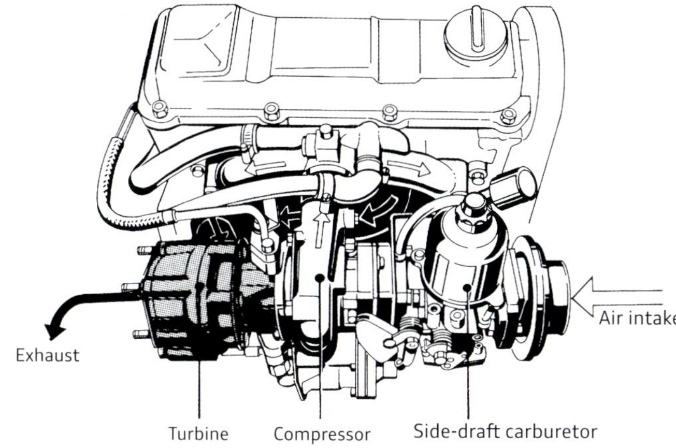

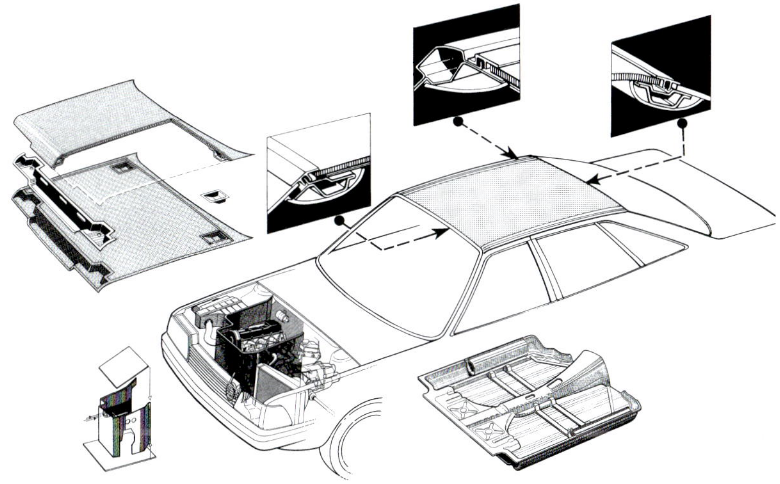

In terms of active safety aspects, Audi relied on front-wheel drive, a negative steering roll radius, diagonally split dual-circuit brakes, and a level-adjustable rear axle, which kept the vehicle in a horizontal position regardless of the load. The driver had access to a vehicle information system that indicated air pressure drop, brake pad wear, and low engine oil level. An onboard computer provided information on time, distance traveled, fuel consumption, and average speed.

The research car was on the Audi stand at the 1981 IAA. The following year, the third generation of the Audi 100 impressively demonstrated how closely the concept car and production model had converged in many technical aspects.

5015-1928
NSU
12

IN-NJ 66

The interior, which concealed innovations such as an early onboard computer, looks rather bizarre from today's perspective. Fabric-covered side panels and windowsill trim—albeit with a more discreet woven pattern—are also found in the third generation of the Audi 100.

"Everything used to be more colorful"—this statement may be true of the 1970s, but by the Eighties, much more muted paint colors were already in vogue.

Fahrleistung:
Audi 100
IN-NR 11
100

Next to the throng of production models, there are rows and rows of studies and show cars from the last decades. In yellow is the Audi TT Offroad Concept, in silver is Audi Cross Coupe quattro, and in terracotta, an early Audi E-tron.

IN TD 1990
IN EL 94

What has now become eight generations of the C series brings together many Audi 100s and A 6s. Among them are rarities such as the white all-electric Audi 100 C4 and the James Bond 200 with Viennese license plates—it is the original car from the movie *The Living Daylights*.

EMBRAGUES
EMBREAGENS
brose

"Avant—The Beautiful Station Wagon." The fourth generation of the Audi 80 included the Lifestyle station wagon in the B segment.

Fahrleistung:
1.000.000
Kilometer
100
Audi 100

Cw 0.198

To the left of the center of the photo is a heavily modified, aerodynamically optimized Audi 80 B2, whose drag coefficient was measured at 0.198 in the Saint Cyr wind tunnel in France.

Above: The polished Audi ASF show car with the first eight-cylinder TDI engine, unveiled at IAA 1993.

quattro

NEW

DIMENSIONS

With the powerful models of the S 2 and S 4 series, Audi had extremely sporty vehicles for every taste in its range at the beginning of the 1990s. With its high-performance engine, the Audi Avant RS2, launched in 1994, was to mark the high point and, at the same time, the end of five-cylinder engines in the company.

Audi RS2 Sedan 1995

Powerplant
Five-cylinder in-line engine, four-stroke with exhaust-driven turbosupercharger

Output
315 hp at 6,500 rpm

Displacement
2,226 cc (135.8 cu. in.)

Maximum speed
262 kph (162.8 mph)

Fuel consumption
12 liters per 100 km (19.60 mpg)

Production life
1994–1995

Total number produced
2 cars

A METEOR IN THE AUDI FIRMAMENT

In March 1989, visitors to the Geneva Motor Show were able to see the new Audi 200 quattro 20 V for the first time. The top model of the series was powered by a newly developed 2.2-liter (134.25-cu. in.) four-valve, turbocharged, five-cylinder engine, which produced 162 kW (220 hp). The legendary engine of the Sport quattro was the inspiration for its design.

From fall 1989, this four-valve turbo also replaced the 147 kW/200 hp two-valve engine in the Audi ur-quattro. The Audi S 2 Coupé followed in August 1990, and in November 1992, Audi announced the S 2 Avant, which could be ordered from February 1993 onward with a version of the basic engine with an increased output of 169 kW (230 hp). It was followed by the Audi S 2 sedan in July 1993. For all these models, "S" stood for "Sporty" and was a reference to the legendary rally version of the Sport quattro, which had caused a sensation as the S 1 with spectacular performances on the rally circuit.

In cooperation with Porsche, the Avant RS2 was created as a further development of the Audi S 2 Avant and was sold exclusively under this name (i.e., without a manufacturer's designation in front of it). The Audi-Porsche consortium (ARGE) was founded specifically for the construction of this high-performance car, which was also entered in the vehicle documents as the manufacturer. The vehicle registration document also contained the rather prosaic type designation P 1.

While Porsche boss Wiedeking regarded the Avant RS2 as a contract manufacturing project within the framework of Porsche Engineering GmbH, Audi board member Kortüm praised the sports car joint venture as the "starting signal for an extensive joint venture." At the International Motor Show in Frankfurt, there was only talk of "cooperation between two manufacturers." In view of the forthcoming model changeover to the Audi A 4, the consortium had planned a production volume of 2,200 vehicles.

Performance upgrades, suspension and brake modifications, and detailed changes to the body, bumpers, and wing mirrors were carried out by Porsche, as was the assembly of the car in the so-called Rösslebau factory in Zuffenhausen. Audi

Compared to the Avant RS2 and its aggressive Porsche-inspired styling, the Audi S 2 sedan looks rather conservative. Even the Avus-designed rims, which have become a style icon, cannot change that. What kind of mark might a limited edition of the "RS2 sedan" at the end of the Audi 80 production series have set? Dreaming is allowed . . .

The halt in production of the B 4 Avant and the B 3 Coupe brought a quick end to the idea of an entire RS2 family of cars. The RS4 sedan from 1994 remained nothing more than an idea.

supplied the complete painted and glazed body, including the reinforced wheel suspensions from the Ingolstadt plant, while the group engine plant in Salzgitter supplied the basic engine without add-on parts. Porsche was responsible for completing the engine with intake manifold, exhaust manifold, and turbocharger, as well as installing the four-piston sports brake system from the Porsche 968 CS, which guaranteed excellent deceleration values in conjunction with brake discs from the Porsche 993 turbo.

With an output of 232 kW (315 hp) at a boost pressure of 1.4 bar (20.3 psi) and a beefy 410 Nm (302 ft.-lb.) of torque at 4,000 rpm, the last and highest factory evolutionary stage of the five-cylinder turbo engines propelled the family-friendly sports sedan to 100 kph (62 mph) in 5.8 seconds and allowed a top speed of 262 kph (162.8 mph)! From March 1994 to August 1995, when production of the basic Audi 80 Avant model ended, ARGE Audi-Porsche produced 2,908 examples of the Avant RS2.

The RS2 sedans built on a trial basis as well as the studies of the RS2 Coupe and the RS4, the adaptation of the drivetrain in an S-4 sedan of the C series (Audi 100), remained largely unknown.

Two sedan prototypes were created at Audi by converting standard S 2 sedans; two further such vehicles were built by a development partner. The 1994 factory vacation marked the end of production of the Audi 80 sedan at Audi, which meant that the basis for a possible RS variant was lost in the truest sense of the word. Since the S 2 sedan had already only sold in limited numbers, just 306 units, any further thoughts about an RS derivative of the sedan were superfluous.

The coupe variant would certainly have had much better sales prospects on the market, but those responsible at Porsche gave it the thumbs down, as an RS2 coupe would possibly have posed a threat to the Zuffenhausen products on the market.

Apart from a few studio photos, no information has survived about the RS4 sedan—not to be confused with the B-series sedan of the same name unveiled in 2000. With the product upgrade of the base model and its renaming from Audi 100 to Audi A 6 in the summer of 1994, quattro GmbH began development of the Audi S 6 plus, a performance-enhanced version of the S 6 4.2 with a 240 kW (326 hp), 4.2-liter, eight-cylinder engine. Today we can only assume that the idea of the RS4 has been shelved.

Audi
Tradition
Audi Tradition

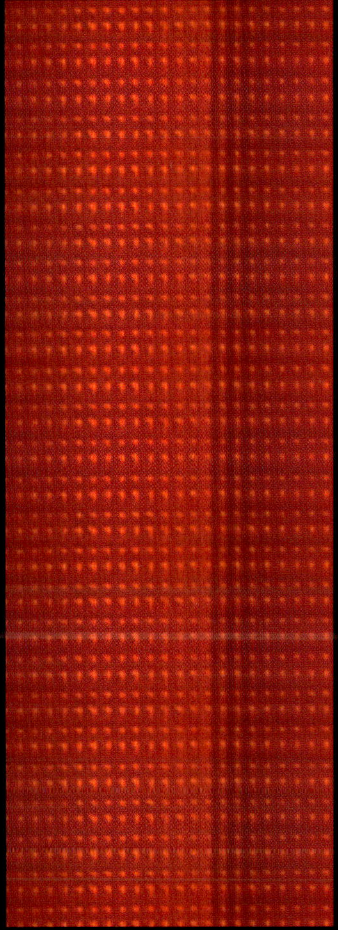

Light and agile, with a powerful engine—the RS2 would have had what it takes to be a big fish in a small pond.

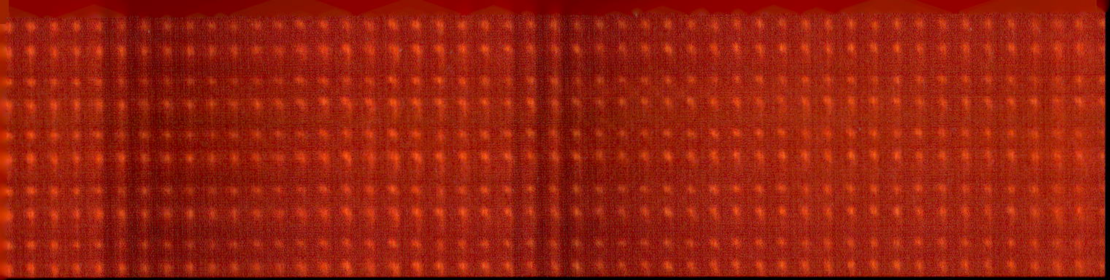

Futuristic music from the past: the first autonomous driving Audi A 8 was made in 2001.

IN TT 647

Design and technical milestones: Audi quattro Spyder from 1991 and Audi A 8 Coupe from the year 1995. With 1,168 vehicles produced, the Audi TT quattro Sport is one of the most desirable early TTs, and the Audi A 2 with fuel cell, tested in 2004.

Audi
Tradition

V6

The first Audi TT is an icon in the company's history. The Audi A 2 hit the market at the wrong time and only later gained the recognition that had been denied it when it was introduced to the market.

Until recently, the papaya-orange A 2 was driven in the internal Neckarsulm factory traffic, which is remarkable because it was a pre-series vehicle built by hand.

From the concept car to the production vehicle, from the Clubsport to a coupe with the powertrain of the Audi R 8 to the autonomously driving "Shelley," an almost zoological variety of TT models is represented.

Audi quattro GmbH
quattro
Audi quattro GmbH

In this photo, the white Audi TT Coupe is the only car that reflects the current state of the series.

Audi V8
1988
Audi ASF

IN RS 4003

The Audi A 3 all-road quattro with matching roof “sarcophagus” remains one of a kind. Sales and marketing did not believe that there were market opportunities for such an elaborate and expensive model.

Al2

ABUS 25t
Audi Q7 V12 TDI

Audi
ceramic

Audi S 1, A 1 e-tron, A 1 quattro, or perhaps an Audi R 8 V10 Spyder instead—those who have the choice are spoiled by choice.

Diesel sports car. Only with magic tricks can the huge V12-TDI from the Q 7 be implanted into the cramped engine compartment of the Audi R 8. An output of 500 hp and 1,000 Nm of torque guarantee "pure driving enjoyment."

There is no shortage of super sports cars. From the R 8 4.2 to the ten-cylinder GT plus, pretty much everything from the series is represented. Of course, an R 8 from customer racing as well—even including a street-legal example!

Movie icon: The Audi RSQ from the science-fiction feature film *I, Robot*, released in 2004

Reverse butterfly doors, xenon lights, and the vehicle's extremely crouching lines give the RSQ an aggressive expression that was still unusual at the time.

Audi A4 B6

The future was yesterday . . . LED rear lights and a digital cockpit have long been standard for the series. Only the control wheels, like the wheel spheres, have yet to make it to the street.

MOBILE

ON TWO WHEELS

NSU produced motorized two-wheelers from the beginning of the twentieth century. The number produced by the company is legion—the one millionth NSU Quickly alone rolled off the production line in 1959.

320

121
120
OSL-1936
NSU

5015-1928
NSU
12

NSU

121
WH-281226

Who counts the types, knows the names? Production of the NSU Quickly alone exceeds one million, and the total number of motorized two-wheelers built in Neckarsulm between 1903 and 1966 is legion.

501 T
1928
NSU
OSL-1936

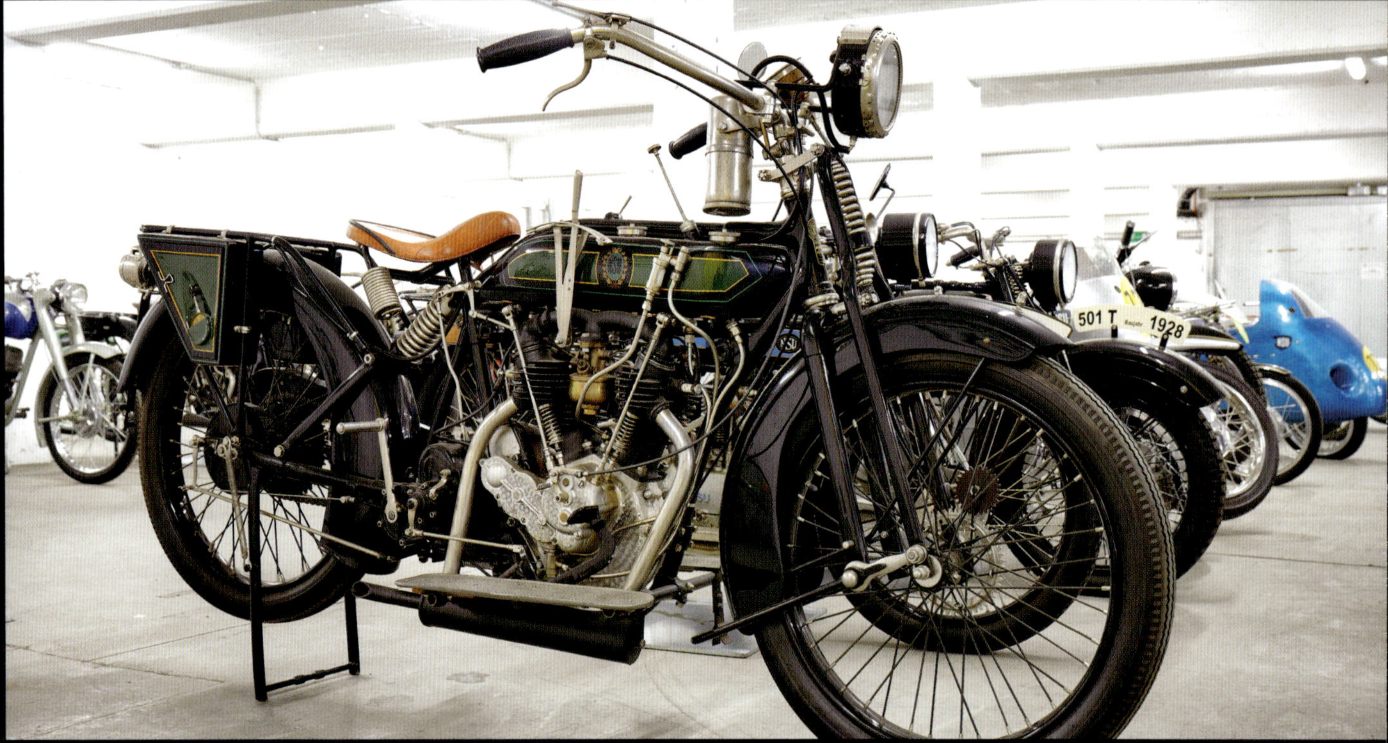

A two-cylinder NSU from the late 1920s. The V engine, with a displacement of 500 cc, delivered 11 hp to the crankshaft.

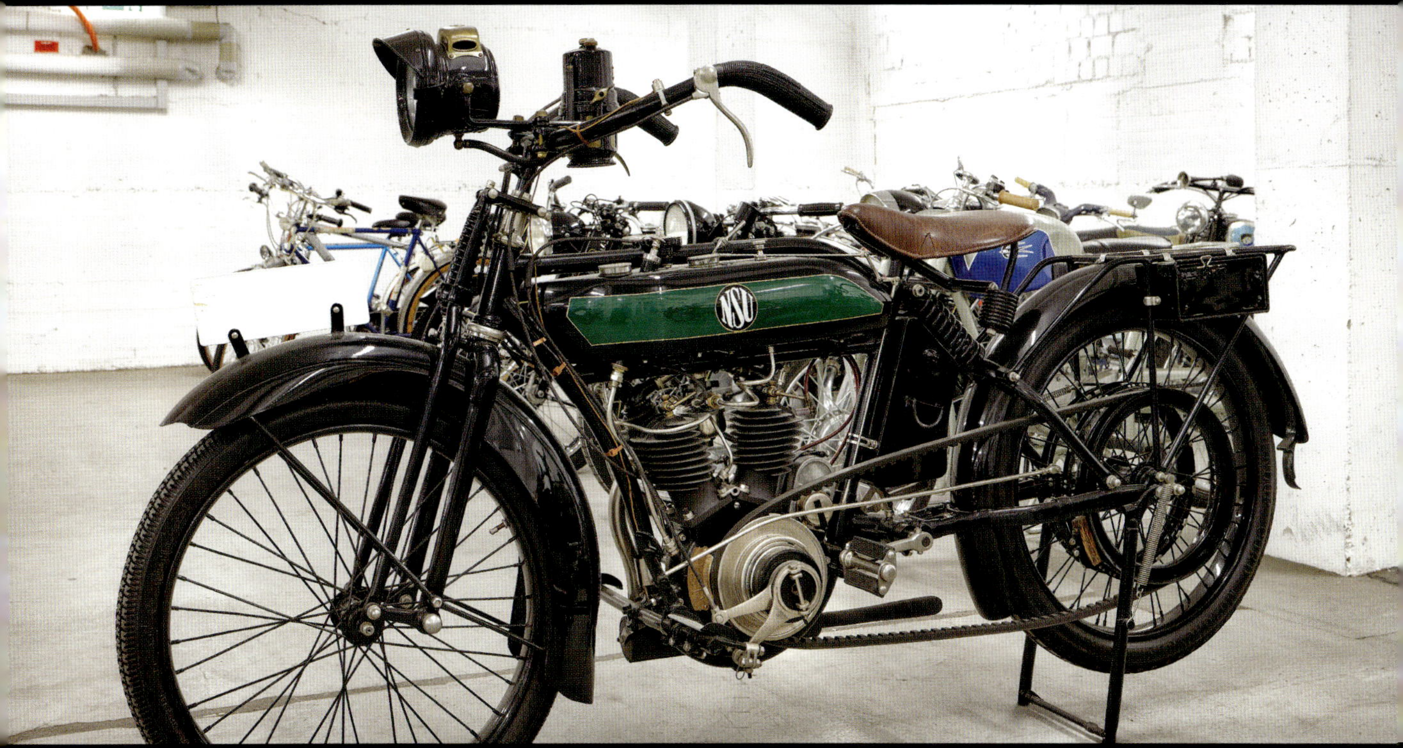
NSU

NSU

NSU

unveiled in 1956.

NSU
TTS

Elective affinity—Friedel Münch transplanted the air-cooled NSU TTS four-cylinder engine into a frame designed by him with a cast electron rear wheel. “Mammut” (Mammoth) was to have been the name of this unrivaled machine at the time. Unfortunately, the Essen-based commercial vehicle manufacturer Krupp had the name Mammut trademarked for a heavy-duty dump truck.

WELL

IN THE RUNNING

The historic vehicle collection houses an almost zoological variety of two- and four-wheeled racing vehicles. Among the motorcycles, DKW and NSU share the respective eras and displacement classes equally. In contrast, the chapter on motorcycle world records is reserved solely for NSU.

The range of racing and sports cars extends from the two oldest, the Audi Type C Alpensieger and the NSU 6/60 PS Kompressorwagen (car with supercharged engine)—which took part in the inaugural Avus race—to current works and privately driven models such as the R 8 LMS GT 3.

Graphic designer Gustav Adolf Baumann had the idea for this "flying lawn chair," with which NSU very successfully pursued world records in various displacement classes in 1954 and 1956.

NSU
5015-1928

NSU

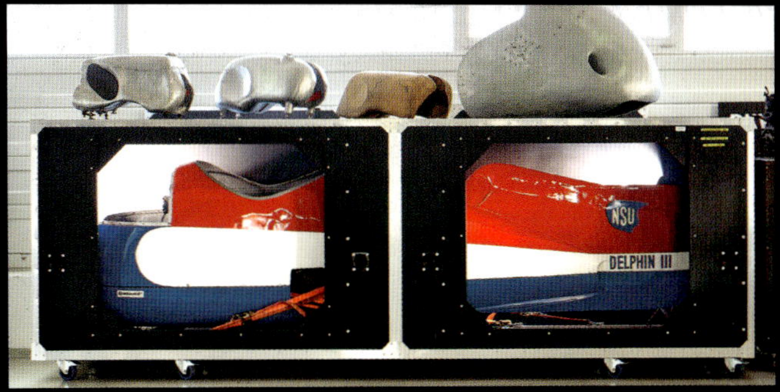

A 500cc, twin-cylinder, supercharged engine producing 110 hp, a closely cut streamlined fairing, and Wilhelm Herz at the controls. In sum they produced the record speed of 339 kph (210.6 mph), achieved at the Bonneville Salt Flats in Utah in August 1956.

NSU
DELPHIN III

The last sixty-five years have left their mark. The dents, however, are not the result of Hertz's collision with a light barrier on the salt flats, as is often reported.

Continental
DELPHIN IV
HERZ
NSU
Kompressormotor
11
167
120
NSU
12
121
120

Rennmax, Rennfox, Sportmax—all three were a guarantee for top places until NSU announced without warning at the end of 1954 that it was giving up factory motorcycle racing.

HERZ

Continental
DELPHIN IV

169

FOX NSU
DEKRA
11
HERZ
NSU

NSU
Continental

NSU
Continental

NSU
Continental
BOSCH
NSU RENN - DIENST
NSU Prinz II (30)
HN SU 235H

SPIESS
TUNING
NSU
Audi
Tradition
NSU RENN -

The NSU TT, built and tuned by old master Siegfried Spiess, was almost impossible to beat on the racetrack. Until their homologation expired, the nimble rear-wheel-drive cars completely dominated their displacement class.

DKW UL 500, 1935–1938

Powerplant
Two-cylinder, double-piston, two-stroke engine

Output
Approx. 48 hp at 5,000 rpm

Displacement
498 cc (30 cu. in.)

Maximum speed
185 kph (114.9 mph)

Fuel consumption
12–15 liters per 100 km (15.7–19.6 mpg), two-stroke mixture 1:15 (l)

Production life
1935–1938

Total production
Unknown

RACING SUCCESS THANKS TO FORCED INDUCTION

On May 1, 1937, the first turbocharged two-cylinder DKW racing machine with a displacement of 500 cc (30.5 cu. in.) premiered at the 24-hour race at Russelheim. The design principle of an auxiliary charge pump under the crankcase, pistons with deflector nose, and liquid cooling was to be constantly refined in detail until 1933—engine output, for example, increased from 26 to 36 hp. Nevertheless, the DKW PRe 500 fell hopelessly behind in terms of performance after 1931.

As early as 1931, the DKW racing department in Zschopau began developing a turbocharged, twin-piston, two-stroke racing engine. In two separate cylinder bores with a common combustion chamber, two pistons worked via a connecting rod on a common stroke journal. The more heavily loaded exhaust piston was connected directly to the main connecting rod. The intake piston sat on an auxiliary connecting rod linked to the main connecting rod. This design, devised by Arnold Zoller at Fafnir in Aachen in 1925, made it possible to achieve an asymmetrical control diagram by lagging the intake piston behind the exhaust piston and, with the exhaust port closed, to overload the engine by around 25% until the intake port was also closed by the piston skirt.

The increase in performance achieved in this way was remarkable, and it was obvious that the two-cylinder machine should also be converted to the new technology. The first version of the UL 500 appeared in 1933. The "U" stood for "U cylinder" (i.e., twin-piston technology), and the "L" stood for "Ladepumpe" (charge pump), the tried-and-tested mechanical forced ventilation. Inside the UL 500, there were now four pistons and an eccentric-jointed charge pump piston measuring almost 100 mm (3.9 in.) in the lower level of the crankcase. In 1934, such an engine was already producing 40 hp at 5,000 rpm and made the single-seater able to reach 175 kph (108.7 mph). Unlike the engine, the frame, fittings, and radiator still looked very much the same for a few years. This changed fundamentally with the introduction of the 1935 models, and in the following years, the focus was increasingly on improving the details.

Intensive work in the wind tunnel beginning in 1936 gave the UL 500 a new fuel tank and the aerodynamically optimized front fender, enabling a more targeted airflow to the radiator, which was almost concealed by the front wheel. At the end of 1936, the 500 was fitted with a rear wheel suspension like that of the 250 models. In the following year, the UL 500 reached its final stage of development with a vertical cylinder

The countless successes achieved by the DKW factory and private drivers contributed significantly to the popularity and high sales figures of the two strokes from Zschopau.

and a radiator that was also mounted vertically in the frame to protect it from crashes and whose effectiveness was improved with the addition of baffles.

These last single-seat 500s produced about 48 hp at 5,000 rpm and reached speeds of up to 190 kph (118 mph). The swan song came in 1938; the 500s were no longer as competitive, especially against the new supercharged BMW. The DKW was hardly used at the factory, leaving this task to private drivers who could purchase "discarded" factory machines.

In addition to individual parts and several cutting motors for exhibition purposes, two UL 500s remain—an experimental machine with rotary valve control, which had to be rebuilt shortly after the war with a 350 chassis, and the machine of a private driver, which was well preserved in Silesia before the end of the war. More than six decades later, it served as a model for the rebuilding of the ready-to-use traditional UL, which occasionally made its bloodcurdling soundscape at historic racing events.

DKW
AUTO UNION

The 500cc single-seater motorcycle is a perfectly crafted, true-to-the-original replica and has already caused a sensation on various racetracks with its bloodcurdling sound.

AUTO UNION
AUTO UNION
AUTO UNION

DKW

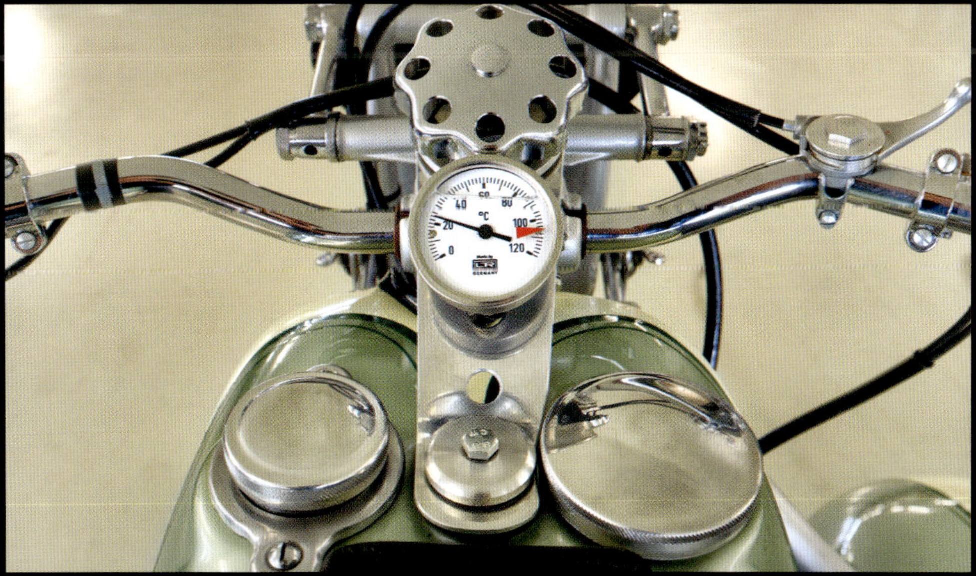

DKW UL 700 Motorcycle-Sidecar Racer, 1936–1937

Powerplant
Two-cylinder, double-piston, two-stroke engine with charging pump

Output
Approx. 50 hp at 5,000 rpm

Displacement
622 cc (38 cu. in.)

Maximum speed
175 kph (108.7 mph)

Fuel consumption
12–15 liters per 100 km (15.68–19.6 mpg), two-stroke mixture 1:15 (L)

Production life
1936–1937

Total production
Unknown

A LOUD POWERHOUSE

In 1935, the DKW racing department developed a four-piston charge pump engine with a displacement of 600 cc (36.6 cu. in.) for the sidecar class up to 600 cc and, in 1936, an additional 700cc engine (42.7cu. in.) for the class up to 1,000 cc, based on the DKW UL 500 solo racing machine, so as to be able to enter the DKW name in motorcycle racing on the winners' lists of the two sidecar classes that were advertised at that time.

The supercharged, liquid-cooled, two-cylinder, twin-piston, two-stroke engine produced 50 hp in the 700cc unit, of which 45 hp was delivered to the rear wheel via a four-speed gearbox and chain. The maximum speed of 5,500 rpm was ridiculously low for a racing engine, but the DKW engines boasted powerful torque and excellent acceleration. The turbocharged high-performance engine had a "healthy thirst"; 20 liters (5.3 gal.) of two-stroke mixture in a mixing ratio of 1:15 to 1:20 ran through the two Amal racing carburetors. Someone who was there at the time commented, "With the big charge pump DKWs, you saw a whirlpool in the tank when the engine was running and the fuel filler cap was removed!" Aptly described, but certainly a little exaggerated . . . a gas can with a prepared mixture, a funnel for quick refueling, and a watering can for the cooling water were as much a part of the basic equipment of every DKW two-cylinder pit crew at all races as the spark plug wrench in the driver's boot. The Bosch racing spark plugs of the time were often unable to cope with the extreme thermal loads, and changing spark plugs, even on the track, was an unpopular but frequent exercise for the charge pump drivers.

Among the motorcycle-sidecar driver teams of Kahrmann/Eder, Braun/Badsching and Schumann/Beer, the DKW sidecar teams proved to be strong, extremely successful opponents against which competitors in both classes were rarely able to score points. It was only logical that in 1936 and 1937, the German championship in the sidecar classes up to 600 cc and up to 1,000 cc went to DKW. In 1937, the European Championship in both classes was added to this series of successes.

Since spectacular accidents had repeatedly occurred in sidecar races, and the top DKW driver Karl Braun was killed in an accident at the Schleizer Dreieck race in August 1937, no more sidecar races were held in Germany after 1938.

Driving the motorcycle-sidecar racers was very hard work. In the fully faired record-setting version, the tall Hans Kahrmann was in dire need of space.

Built in 1936, this motorcycle-sidecar from the Audi AG collection is the only one to have survived the war years. It was driven by Hans Schumann with co-driver Julius Beer until the end of the 1937 season; both won the European Championship in the sidecar class up to 1,000 cc in 1937. After that, all traces are lost in the darkness of events.

In the postwar period, the UL 700 turned up at Auto Union GmbH in ways that can no longer be traced. For a time, it is said to have been on display in the administration building of the Düsseldorf plant and the "Haus der Technik" (Technology Center) there. After DKW in Ingolstadt finally gave up motorcycle production in 1958, the motorcycle was initially transferred to Zweirad Union in Neumarkt. After it was taken over by Nuremberg-based Hercules-Werke GmbH in 1966, the rare piece was initially kept in Nuremberg and was eventually loaned to the Zweirad-Museum in Neckarsulm for the long term.

A few years ago, Audi Tradition commissioned a specialist for DKW racing motorcycles based in Saxony to restore it to a roadworthy and usable condition. The loud powerhouse has already completed its rollout, but its first appearance on historic ground is still to come.

MOTANOL
Schmierdienst
83
2

DKW
SHELL
MOTANOL
83
2

Schmierdiens
83
TDI

TDI
MICHELIN
BOSCH
MAHLE

Audi ultra
Audi e-tron quattro
TDI
MAHLE
BOSCH
MICHELIN
LEUNA
83
Audi Sport
Castrol
HB
international

Audi and Le Mans are linked by a seventeen-year history of success, with no less than thirteen victories at the track on the Sarthe River.

2
MAHLE
BOSCH

The Le Mans cars are arranged in a row according to the years they were used and thus allow a unique overview of their evolutionary history.

What appear to be bugs splattered on the front of the cars are in fact the marks left by rubber particles.

Stuck
BOSCH
HY
ORIS
Swiss Watches
MICHELIN
DUNLOP
A4

Among the vehicles from the first two years of operation, Crocodile, designed by Frank Lamberty, stands out. The four-wheeled reminder of the movie *Crocodile Dundee* was used in the Millennium Race in Adelaide, Australia, at the end of 2000.

8
Panasonic Car Audio
Infineon technologies
MICHELIN
1
Infineon
MAHLE

AUDI NSU
SHELL
SHELL AUTOOELE
Audi Sport
Castrol
Hankook
8
Shell
MICHELIN

AUDI NSU
LEUNA
24 HEURES DU MANS
8
Infineon
Infineon
MICHELIN
MICHELIN

SHELL

8
TAKARA
MICHELIN

V8
V8

SCHAEFFLER
gratuliert
Martin Tomczyk
BOSCH
Tomczyk
Audi Sport
DEKRA
14
ADAC
FAG
LUK
INA
Hankook
Audi e-tron quattro
TDI

DTM, LMP, STW, Trans Am, and Rallye world championships—a condensed overview of almost forty years of motorsport history under the symbol of the four rings.

Audi Sport
Audi Sport
nothelle tuning
Veedol
SCHRICK
163
nothelle tuning

SHELL
LEUNA
Audi Sport
Audi Sport
Castrol
quattro
SKF
BOGE
MICHELIN
HB International
2
MICHELIN
Audi Sport
Castrol
HB International
MICHELIN

Marlboro
Safari Rally Kenya
7
EPSON
HB
international
H.MIKKOLA
A.HERTZ
MICHELIN
Audi Sport
TEXACO
BOGE
SHELL AUTOOELE

SHELL
Continental
LEUNA
SONAX
44
Audi Sport
BOSCH LÖBRO DUNLOP
Shell
TECHNIK
KONI
DUNLOP
BBS
RECARO
Castrol
BOSCH

HB AUDI TEAM
MICHELIN
Castrol
HB AUDI TEAM
MICHELIN
HB AUDI TEAM
Castrol
MICHELIN

Audi quattro
SONAX
Shell
telcon
Shell
DUNLOP
BOSCH
Audi quattro
SONAX
DUNLOP
Shell
Shell
BOSCH
BOSCH
Philips Car Systems
4
DUNLOP
Castrol
A4
Castrol

There is something for every preference: evolution of the Rallye quattros, the path from the DTM V8 to the master of the STW, or an actual Customer Racing R 8 LMS.

AUDI NSU
Audi Sport
Castrol
HANKOOK
ENT
Audi Sport
Marlboro
Safari Rally Kenya
EPSON
HB
international
IN YV 71
MICHELIN
TDI

D

TEXACO
SKF
quattro
MICHELIN
EN YV 71
D

quattro
only

PIRELLI
Hella
CHAMPION
Triplex
MINTEX
80er
B.CEDERBERG
Audi Sport

Oh, if only they could speak. The quattros that flustered the circuits at the RAC Rallye, the Rallye Monte Carlo, the Acropolis Rallye, and countless other world championship races or circuits in the US and Europe.

R18
Auto Union
Typ A
Audi quattro
4
Audi
quattro
GOODYEAR
BOSCH
GOODYEAR
BBS
BBS
Shell
Shell

Auto Union
Typ A
R18
Audi quattro

Wiper
Reverse
Off
Main
Ignition
OBR
Fog
Start
On
Turn
Highbeam
Pump
REV
Reset
Heater
Neutral
Pump
Data
E
LIVE
MODE
12
KCLR
OFF

As you can see, the driver of a Le Mans car had tunnel vision and could see next to nothing. The screen at the top of the windshield served as a rear-view mirror.

R8 5.2 quattr

The Audi Avus quattro, Audi ASF, and the high-gloss Audi A 2, the latest polished pearls in the vehicle collection

Other Schiffer Books on Related Subjects:
Mercedes-Benz C 111: The Definitive History of the Mysterious Supercar That Never Was, Gerhard Heidbrink and Joachim Hack, ISBN 978-0-7643-6900-1
McLaren: The Road Cars, 2010–2024, Kyle Fortune, ISBN 978-0-7643-6731-1
Alfa Romeo: An Illustrated History, 1910–2020, Christian Schön, ed., ISBN 978-0-7643-6730-4

Originally published as *Einblicke die Fahrzeugsammlung der Audi AG*, ©2022 Auto Union GmbH, by Delius Klasing Verlag, Bielefeld.
Translated from the German by David Johnston.

Library of Congress Control Number: 2025939838

Edited by Ralf Friese and Hanno Vienken
Designed by *ö.konzept Zwickau, Matthias Kaluza, Sven Rahnefeld
Cover design by Danielle Farmer
Production design by Kate North
Photography: Stefan Warter
Text: Ralf Friese

Type set in Audi Type Extended Bold/Extended Normal/Normal

ISBN: 978-0-7643-7102-8
Printed in China

10 9 8 7 6 5 4 3 2 1

MIX
Paper | Supporting responsible forestry
FSC® C104723

Published by Schiffer Publishing, Ltd.
4880 Lower Valley Road
Atglen, PA 19310
Phone: (610) 593-1777; Fax: (610) 593-2002
Email: Info@schifferbooks.com
Web: www.schifferbooks.com